Transport Infrastructure in Time, Scope and Scale

Björn Hasselgren

Transport Infrastructure in Time, Scope and Scale

An Economic History and Evolutionary Perspective

palgrave
macmillan

Björn Hasselgren
Uppsala University
Uppsala, Sweden

ISBN 978-3-319-79053-4 ISBN 978-3-319-79054-1 (eBook)
https://doi.org/10.1007/978-3-319-79054-1

Library of Congress Control Number: 2018940759

Printed on acid-free paper

This Palgrave Macmillan imprint is published by the registered company Springer International Publishing AG part of Springer Nature
The registered company address is: Gewerbestrasse 11, 6330 Cham, Switzerland

For Marie

Contents

1	**Government Ownership of Roads and Railroads—Why?**	**1**
	1.1 The Traditional Arguments for Government Intervention and the Challenges to These Arguments	1
	References	7
2	**Theoretical Background**	**9**
	2.1 Methods, Sources, and the Research Process	9
	2.1.1 Methods and Sources	9
	2.1.2 The Research Process behind this Book	13
	2.2 Some Perspectives on Transport Infrastructure	15
	2.2.1 The Transport System—Functions and Temporal Perspectives	15
	2.2.2 Functional Roles and Spatial Dimensions	18
	References	22
3	**Economic Theory and Transport Infrastructure**	**25**
	3.1 Introduction	25
	3.2 Neoclassical Theories and Welfare Economics	32
	3.2.1 Natural Monopoly Theory	32
	3.2.2 A Dichotomy of Failure and Success	35

3.2.3 Neoclassical Theory and Market Failure Views 36
3.3 Institutional Theory and Organizational Focus 39
3.3.1 Stable and Dynamic Transaction Costs 42
3.3.2 Hybrid Organizations—The Middle Way? 45
3.4 A Coevolutionary Development Approach 46
References 52

4 Planning and Coordination of Transport Infrastructure 57
4.1 Knowledge and Coordination 59
4.2 The Spatial Dimension 67
4.3 Recent Trends in the EU and the USA 68
References 75

5 Sweden's Transport Infrastructure History—Coevolution and Conflict 79
5.1 Transport Infrastructure Chronology 1939–2010, a Coevolutionary Perspective 79
5.1.1 1939–1963—Nationalization and Professionalization 81
5.1.2 1963–1988 and 1989—The Present—Social Marginal Costs or Not? 87
5.1.3 Conclusions 90
5.2 Marginal Cost Controversies—Different Views on Financing 90
5.2.1 Financing Principles 90
5.2.2 A Government Dilemma and Coase's View 91
5.2.3 A Marginal Cost Controversy in Swedish Transport Infrastructure Policy? 97
5.2.4 Reasons for the Change in Policies 98
5.2.5 Incentives for Efficiency Changed? 101
References 103

Concluding Remarks 107

References 109

Index 119

List of Figures

Fig. 1.1	The traditional arguments for government intervention in transport infrastructure	5
Fig. 2.1	Government's functional roles in transport infrastructure and different spatial levels	19
Fig. 3.1	Neoclassical and institutional theories—some features (*Source* Based on Klein (1998) and Huerta de Soto (2010))	27
Fig. 3.2	Core theoretical approaches and additional approaches	30
Fig. 3.3	The theoretical paradigms and applications of these in transport infrastructure	31
Fig. 3.4	Public and private goods and models for provision of these services and goods	35
Fig. 3.5	Transaction costs and cases for hierarchy or market organization (*Source* Williamson 1981, 1999)	43
Fig. 3.6	Three areas of managerial practices and organisational forms over time (*Source* Based on Langlois (2003), adjusted)	44
Fig. 3.7	Development of transport infrastructure systems—a coevolutionary approach	49
Fig. 4.1	Four modes of transport infrastructure planning	64
Fig. 4.2	Centralization and decentralization of transport infrastructure issues	70

Fig. 4.3 Coordination through spontaneous ordering—a possible way ahead? 74

Fig. 5.1 Transport infrastructure development chronology 1939–2010, a coevolutionary perspective (*Source* Hasselgren 2013d) 80

Fig. 5.2 An influence from technology and economic factors explain the nationalization 84

Fig. 5.3 Postwar transport policies were influenced by available resources in relation to demand for new roads 86

Fig. 5.4 Since the 1970s welfare economics and politics have increasingly influenced transport infrastructure policies 89

Fig. 5.5 Coase and Pigou/Hotelling—different views on cost coverage and financing 95

Fig. 5.6 The marginal cost controversy in Sweden's transport infrastructure policy 102

Introduction

Transport infrastructure systems are part of our everyday life to such a high extent that we often take them for granted. We travel to work or school, for business or pleasure. Goods are transported in different speed and geographies. The modern way of organizing our life, societies, and economies has become more and more dependent on transportation and transportation and transport infrastructure has become an important part of the economy in itself.

In a historic perspective, transportation has always been an important aspect of human life. Exchange of goods and travel for different purposes, peaceful or in war, has driven the interest of moving people and things since ancient times. Successive innovations have led to an evolving transportation system with higher and higher speed, outreach, and interconnectivity.

For a long time, transportation systems were mainly decoupled and decentralized in their structure. Carriages, maritime vessels, and feet dominated as transportation means. Roads existed but the quality of roads, even if such exited for example in the Roman Empire, was generally poor. Kings and central powers often had an interest in keeping some kind of national roads to support transport needs of a central government, but the building and maintenance of roads was often a duty of local authorities or farmers, etc. Only in cities existed some kind of network of streets and roads that allowed for a more developed transportation, and the quality was poor even here. Harbors and ships represented perhaps the most developed of transportation systems with technologically advanced vessels.

A drastic change occurred with the advent of inner waterways/canals, railway technology, and motorized road vehicles. Suddenly something like a modern transportation infrastructure was constructed. Canals and railroads could be organized in local and centralized structures but they were based on considerable new investments in physical fixed assets that had to be maintained and operated in a coordinated way to produce transport services that could generate enough cash flow to pay back the costs of the systems. As motor vehicles were developed from the 1910s and onward, the need for an upgraded road network with better surface and quality standard than before was necessary, even if plank roads exemplified an innovation in quality and performance in the nineteenth century which gave a flavor of what was coming.

Air transportation, which is still perhaps in its infancy, grew in parallel with modern road transportation. The introduction of modern motor technologies made flying vessels possible and long-distance connectivity primarily for passengers much faster. As a structural system, air transport resembles maritime transportation more than roads and railroads. Even if airports represent major investments in a local economy, the fixed assets necessary for air transport are limited in comparison. Perhaps air transport systems are currently evolving into something more like coherent systems, with more advanced air-traffic control and increased need for coordination with a higher capacity utilization in the system. This might become an area for development of new theories and thinking, similar to what happened for roads and railroads a hundred and fifty years ago.

Much of the modern discussion on transport infrastructure, its organization, financing, and use grew from the time of the introduction of railways and modern road vehicles. In this book, the primary focus is set on the time from the 1840s and up to our present time. Roads and railroads are the two transportation modes that are focused. The reason for this is that these two transportation modes have been in focus of the public debate and the interest in academia over questions related to organization, financing, and operations.

Another reason for choosing roads and railroads as a study object here is that these two infrastructure systems have to a large extent been owned, financed and operated by governments, while maritime transportation- and air transportation-related infrastructure assets have been owned to a higher extent by actors in the private sector and funded by user charges. A major question here is why it is that governments still do own, finance, and operate roads and railroads, even if similar infrastructure systems in other areas of the economy have gradually been transferred to private-sector organization.

The hypothesis behind the research project, my Ph.D. project, which is the basis of this book, was that this had to do with the strength of economic theorizing and views "in the public domain" including politics, that government ownership and organization of roads and railroads is the "natural" thing. Privatization of these systems has often been seen as impossible or to be countering conventional wisdom in general, no matter what the original basis for the argumentation was.

In order to understand and analyze the long-term development of a societal and economic system like transport infrastructure, it is helpful to apply some theoretical and methodological framework to structure the multitude of data speaking about the time, scope, and scale propensities of transportation and transport infrastructure. This framework in this book and the research behind it has to a large extent been institutional theory and a coevolutionary perspective. Here, different subsystems and factors in the economy are identified and used as a base for structuring data over time.

Coevolution signifies a view on the development of the infrastructure systems where different factors and circumstances interact, sometimes to support a line of evolution, sometimes in competition. The perspective will be further explained below. Institutional theory is here seen as a set of theories where, among other included interests, an organizational perspective is put to the fore. Here primarily on the level of the organizational units responsible for the management of transport infrastructure assets, such as government agencies or private-sector corporations.

The book focuses on the development of roads and railroads in Western Europe and the USA while Sweden is the study object of a longitudinal analysis of transport infrastructure policy from the 1930s to the 2010s as regards the coevolutionary perspective and the influence economic theories has had on policy formation. Sweden is interesting as a study object since it is a country which went through a marketization process in the 1980s–1990s where deregulation and increased competition in many former government-controlled sectors was at the core of politics. Roads and railroads have though remained in the hands of the government. The main question is why and how we can understand the development.

Discussing transport infrastructure policy and reality over time two other dimensions are covered; planning vs. markets and coordination vs. spontaneity. These are themes that have been widely discussed in planning literature and in economics. Here, a Hayekian Austrian perspective is contrasted against a more centralist neoclassical perspective. It is argued that this gives deepened understanding of the organizational challenges and outcomes in relation to transport infrastructure.

The book is divided into five chapters. In Chapter 1, an introduction into the subject of government ownership of transport infrastructure assets is given. Some of the traditional arguments for and against government intervention into the transport infrastructure sector are reflected.

Chapter 2 goes into some of the theories behind the analysis and discussion in the book. Transport infrastructure as systems with an outreach over time, scope, and scale is sketched. Furthermore the research process leading to this book is presented, and some of the methodological aspects of the research project.

Chapter 3 discusses how economic theories in relation to transport infrastructure systems have influenced the way we discuss and analyze these systems. Neoclassical economics is contrasted against an institutional and organizational perspective. The role of transaction costs over time. Scale and scope of the systems is discussed and a coevolutionary institutional view on the development of transport infrastructure systems over time presented.

Chapter 4 focuses on planning theory and planning paradigms in relation to transport infrastructure. Here, the ability of planners in the public sector to access information, also discussed as knowledge, is contrasted to a decentralized view where knowledge is an outcome of a learning process more than an input. How planning or spontaneous market interaction relates to coordination and thus, resource allocation is also a theme as well as planning on different spatial levels in the economy. An application to current trends in planning of transport infrastructure in the USA and EU ends the chapter.

Chapter 5 entails two examples of applications of the theories outlined in Chapters 2–4. First, a chronological description of transport infrastructure policy in Sweden from the 1930s to the 2010s is presented based on the coevolutionary perspective. Second, Swedish financing and management policies in the transport infrastructure sector from the Second World War is analyzed, based on the application of marginal cost or full cost coverage policies. Both these policies have been in use in Sweden since the 1940s. The chapter discusses how the different policy settings have affected resource allocation and efficiency in the sector.

Finally, the chapter gives some concluding remarks on the past, present, and future of transport infrastructure systems.

1
Government Ownership of Roads and Railroads—Why?

1.1 The Traditional Arguments for Government Intervention and the Challenges to These Arguments

Transport infrastructure systems of different kinds are signified by heavy and long-term investments and often connected to different views on the strategic development of economies, nations, and the way we live. Therefore, transport infrastructure over time has been an area for interest by governments, and for other actors.

In Western Europe and many other countries, government's interest in these systems has a long tradition from medieval times to the development of postal services in the seventeenth century and up to the modern industrial era, when transport volumes started to grow and new technology made transportation cheaper and faster. The long tradition of government regulations around the construction and maintenance of roads can be exemplified through the inclusion of these in the very first legal texts from the thirteenth and fourteenth centuries in Sweden (Bulletinen 2012).

B. Hasselgren, *Transport Infrastructure in Time, Scope and Scale*,
https://doi.org/10.1007/978-3-319-79054-1_1

The industrial revolution increased the demand for transport infrastructure. Starting in the earliest industrialized country, Britain, and quickly spreading around the Western world new transport infrastructure was developed. This meant that the scope of transport infrastructure functionality and operations also changed quickly. A deepened competition between different transport modes evolved and the scale of transport infrastructure assets also increased from local systems to more national structures. Railroad corporations, perhaps apart from inland waterways and shipping organizations like the East Indian Companies, were among the first mega-organizations to evolve (Chandler 1977, 1990).

Three phases in the development of transport infrastructure can generally be identified in most countries, according to Millward (2005, 2011). The first is the entrepreneurial phase where private corporations are active in shaping the first systems. Governments started to become more interested in the systems as they grew into large financial and influential systems with network effects that were vital to government control. Theories on whether governments should intervene in order to regulate both the provision of transport services and the price level were developed during the nineteenth century. These theories have had a persistent influence on the views around transport infrastructure development, financing, regulation, and ownership.

A wave of nationalizations during the mid-1900s marked the next major phase in the development of transport infrastructure, according to Millward. Railroads and roads on the national level were brought under government ownership in many countries, partly as a response to the lack of profitability of railroads and a perceived need to economize in order to reap large-scale effects in the systems.

The third phase in this development came in the 1980s when a general deregulation and liberalization took place in many countries. This primarily included liberalization and market openings in transportation, while the organization and regulation of transport infrastructure were more stable. In some countries, and Sweden is a good example, a separation of the railroad system into infrastructure and transportation services was implemented, which was the start of further deregulation. EU policies in the transport policy area have also supported the further process of strengthening reform and deregulation in the sector.

Recently has there been a tendency for weakening momentum in these policies, as exemplified by Johnson and Turner (2007). Whether the outcomes of the sustained financial crisis in many countries in the EU will bring further or less EU-led coordination is still to be seen. Initiatives from the EU since some years back such as the focus on developing Core Network Corridors (CNSs) and the introduction of novel financing tools following the financial crisis of 2008–2009 seem to signal something of a new era in relation to transport infrastructure coordination in the EU, but outcomes are still uncertain.

In economics literature, there has been a discussion around transport infrastructure systems more closely based on the division of services and goods in an economy in the categories of public and private goods. A wide scholarly debate, but also a more practical discussion, on the cooperation between actors in the public and private sectors when it comes to transport infrastructure provision and operations has played out, and still continues.

The prevailing strengthened role of the government in the transport infrastructure sector can also be discussed as an example of path dependency, which can be interpreted both in a broader and in a narrower form, as suggested by Piersson (2000). The broader form views causality between present and earlier stages as fundamental. In contrast, the narrower view is more based on the presence of sunk costs, meaning that as a development starts it is costly to change to another development path or technology. The fact that government ownership of transport infrastructure has been essentially unchallenged might in this light be understood both as a consequence of the influence of economic and political arguments favoring prevailing government engagement and as an effect of the substantial investment necessary for any organization to challenge the government with competing systems.

Other reasons for the government to take on a more active role in the transport infrastructure sector have been a political interest in influencing regional development, distributional effects in general, and the government's interest to control land use and rights of way in connection with transport infrastructure planning and construction.

There has also been a view in political discussions that regional development and regional growth have been positively connected to transport infrastructure systems, and that transport infrastructure policy can be used as an efficient means of reaching the fulfillment of regional policy and growth objectives. An early example of this view is the doctoral thesis by Heckscher (1907), analyzing the importance of railroad construction in Sweden in the nineteenth century for regional growth.

In addition to this, governments have generally had an interest in controlling the territory (physically) via the transport systems, as a necessary means for the core functions of the government (police, defense, tax collection, and education) to be carried out. These broad policy reasons for government intervention have often been included in the natural monopoly arguments without clear distinctions between the different arguments. A similar description of arguments in favor of government intervention in many industries with parallel features has been presented by Bogart (2009) and Clifton et al. (2011).

Clifton et al. have pointed to economic, military, redistributional, and social motivations for government intervention in the systems. Some of the arguments that are often raised in this discussion, arguments which have over time often been intertwined without clear separation, are depicted in Fig. 1.1. The varying importance and strength of these arguments over time in forming the Swedish government's policies around transport infrastructure has been discussed by Hasselgren (2013).

Today, many of these arguments for national government intervention seem to be less relevant in the arguments for sustained government ownership and the financing of transport infrastructure. The possibility to introduce road and railroad pricing based on new payment technology solutions have made it less necessary to lean on taxation of fuel as the main source of funding of roads. On the one hand, this is a threat to the government's revenues from road-related taxes; however, on the other hand, it is a possibility. For railroads specifically, more developed charging for different users (operators) of the railroads can be introduced. There is also a possibility to add cost-based elements to the prices, whereby proxies for external cost effects of transport systems can be included in the pricing system.

New technology thus has made the introduction of market structures in the transport infrastructure sector and the financing of private

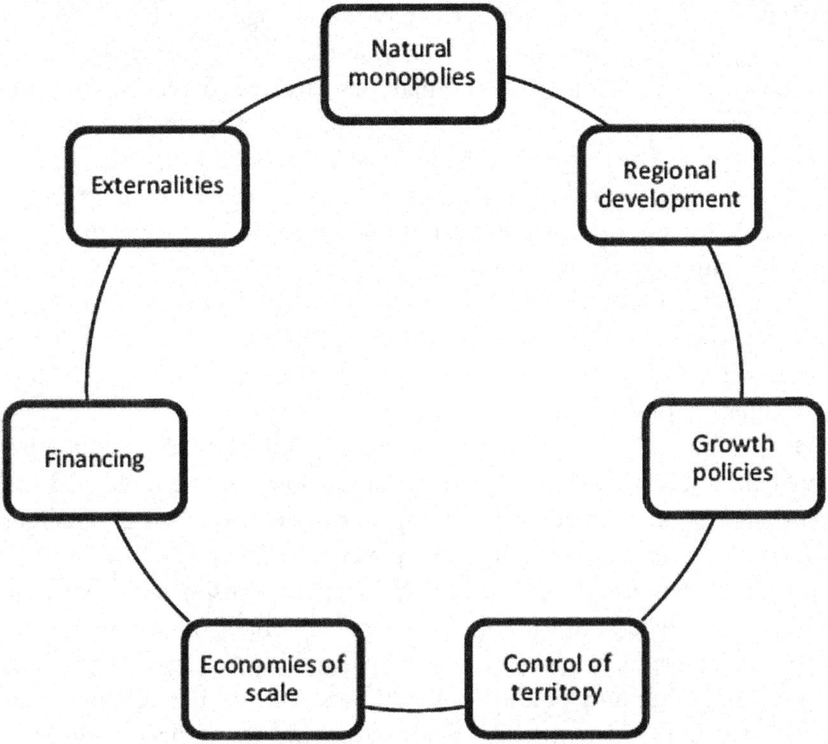

Fig. 1.1 The traditional arguments for government intervention in transport infrastructure

corporations in transport infrastructure more likely than before. This also weakens one of the core traditional arguments in favor of government intervention in the area.

Klein (2012) discusses technological change and its effects on government intervention such as measures used for the alleviation of the effects of natural monopolies. Klein focuses on the fact that technological development could weaken arguments for government intervention, as technology makes payment systems for roads possible to implement. Yet, it could be argued that technological development allows for increased government regulation and intervention. The government will simply be in a position to control and regulate more aspects of the economy as information collection and more effective control measures are developed. Klein suggests that technological change will also likely make the economy more complex. An example could be the development of Information Technology (IT), which has enabled the cheaper collection of information but at the same time made society and the economy more complex. The knowledge frontier seems to be a target that is moving all the time. Even if technology is improving there might, therefore, be good reasons to question the viability of government intervention.

The changing distribution of decision rights and competence between different spatial levels in most countries, with tendencies for strengthening local and regional levels, combined with more ambitious coordination at the international level in the EU has also challenged the government's role as infrastructure provider. Scale effects are of course still important in the sector, but it is perhaps more likely to find them now at the international level and perhaps also at the regional and local level than before. This development speaks in favor of a future challenge of the national level and the national government.

It can of course also be discussed whether transport infrastructure policy is an efficient means of furthering regional policy and regional growth objectives. For example, is there anything other than (or wider than) time saving and quality improvement effects that could be connected to new investments in infrastructure and upgrading of the existing infrastructure through reinvestment? Growth and positive regional growth effects in relation to new infrastructure might also be more a case of redistribution between different locations than pure net growth effects. This has in fact been one of the criticisms toward local taxes such as local VAT tax, which is sometimes a means of financing transport infrastructure in those countries where such measures are used. The counterargument toward these new financing methods is that they tend to lead to limited net tax revenue since they primarily cover redistribution of economic activity in connection with infrastructure investments. These wider economic impacts (or benefits) of transport infrastructure investments are discussed for example by Vickerman (2007) and is an area of current methodological development.

One aspect of the decreased strength of the arguments for prolonged government intervention is the decline of the center-periphery model as a road map for the organization of institutions and the functioning of the state. This discussion was already raised in the 1970s by Schön (1971). There are more frequent threats to the traditional roles and settings of the central government and the regional and local parts of systems, which necessitates new governance practices in a number of areas of business life and in the public sector.

Schön discussed the role of infrastructure as a means for the stable state to function in order to transport goods and people, but also for information flows to work. To control infrastructure was thus part of the (central) stable state's strategy to remain in power in the late nineteenth and early twentieth centuries. However, since the late twentieth century, new information and communication channels were seen as threats to the stable state. The old systems might have become obsolete and the need for investments in the old physical systems might become too strong of a burden for the state.

Consequently, many of the traditional arguments in favor of government intervention seem to be questioned today. Whether this exemplifies a stronger challenge to the government's role than at many times before, or is primarily another example of a challenge that will be met by the government adjusting its role to the new situation, is still to be seen. In order to better understand transport infrastructure and its role in the economies and in the development of modern societies, a perspective combining aspects of time, scope, and scale is important. This book develops these themes with examples both of theoretical discussions and practical applications.

References

Bogart, D. (2009). Nationalizations and the Development of Transport Systems: Cross-Country Evidence from Railroad Networks, 1860–1912. *The Journal of Economic History, 69*(01), 202–237.

Bulletinen. (2012). Nr 2, 2012, Enskild väghållning i svensk historia 1200–2010, based on Blomkvist, Pär Om förvaltning av gemensamma resurser: Enskild väghållning och allmänningens dilemma i svensk historia 1200–2010 (Managing Common Pool Resources: Road Keeping and the Dilemma of the Commons in Swedish History 1200–2010), Division of

Industrial Dynamics, Royal Institute of Technology, Stockholm (Stockholm 2010), TRITA-IEO 2010:06.

Chandler, A. D. (1977). *The Visible Hand: The Managerial Revolution in American Business*. Cambridge, MA, USA: The Belknap Press of Harvard University Press.

Chandler, A. D. (1990). *Scale and Scope: The Dynamics of Industrial Capitalism*. Cambridge, MA, USA: The Belknap Press of Harvard University Press.

Clifton, J., Lanthier, P., & Schröter, H. (2011). Regulating and Deregulating the Public Utilities 1830–2010. *Business History, 53*(5), 659–672.

Hasselgren, B. (2013). The Swedish Government as Owner of Transport Infrastructure. Policy Formation from the 1930s to the 2010s. *Scandinavian Journal of Public Administration, 16*(4), 49–71.

Heckscher, E. F. (1907). *Till belysning af jernvägarnas betydelse för Sveriges ekonomiska utveckling*. Stockholm: Centraltryckeriet.

Johnson, D., & Turner, C. (2007). *Strategy and Policy for Trans-European Networks*. Houndmills, Basingstoke, Hampshire: Palgrave Macmillan.

Klein, D. B. (2012). *Knowledge and Coordination—A Liberal Interpretation*. New York: Oxford University Press Inc.

Millward, R. (2005). *Private and Public Enterprise in Europe*. UK: Cambridge University Press.

Millward, R. (2011). Public Enterprise in the Modern Western World: An Historical Analysis. *Annals of Public and Cooperative Economics, 82*(4), 378–398.

Pierson, P. (2000). Increasing Returns, Path Dependence and the Study of Politics. *The American Political Science Review, 94*(2), 251–267.

Schön, D. A. (1971). *Beyond the Stable State. Public and Private Learning in a Changing Society*. London: Temple Smith.

Vickerman, R. (2007). *Recent Evolution of Research into the Wider Economic Benefits of Transport Infrastructure Investments* (OECD/ITF Joint Transport Research Centre Discussion Papers No. 2007/9). OECD Publishing.

2
Theoretical Background

2.1 Methods, Sources, and the Research Process

2.1.1 Methods and Sources

Three different perspectives are important when analyzing the government's role for transport infrastructure and the development of the role over time. These comparisons are: (a) over time; (b) between different geographical levels and; and (c) to some extent between different infrastructure sectors.

The practical examples in this book are based on empirical data gathering from four different sources:

- Reports from government committees and the government's proposals to the Swedish Parliament for decisions to be taken. Also studied were reports from Parliament's different standing committees for transport infrastructure issues.

B. Hasselgren, *Transport Infrastructure in Time, Scope and Scale*,
https://doi.org/10.1007/978-3-319-79054-1_2

- Official documents from governments and Parliaments in other countries, mainly the USA, UK, Germany, Finland, Norway, Denmark, and the EU.
- Reports (academic and other) covering different issues in relation to transport infrastructure from public and private institutions and organizations.
- Interviews with senior officials in government ministries, from the responsible transport agencies, and with a large number of officials.

An extensive number of reports, government bills and proposals, and parliamentary documents have been studied during this project, primarily in the Parliamentary Library in Stockholm. These documents cover the time from the late 1800s to the 2010s. A complete literature list covering these sources is included in Hasselgren (2013a).

The intertemporal comparison provides a historical perspective primarily on the development of the government's role in the road and railroad sectors in Sweden. Here, the starting point is the decision processes in the late 1930s and early 1940s when the government nationalized locally and privately owned and managed rural roads and railroads. The focus is to clarify which arguments were used and most influential in the nationalization process and whether they are still relevant today. With regard to railroads, these issues have been studied by many. Alvfors (1977), Andersson-Skog (1993), and Ottosson (1997) provide interesting insights into the processes in Sweden and in relation to other countries. Blomkvist (2001) is one of the scholars who has analyzed the growth of the modern road system since the early twentieth century.

As a background to the analysis, references are also made to earlier time periods. For example, the growth of the railroad system is described with references to the decisions in the mid- and late nineteenth century by the Swedish government and by its Parliament. Kaijser (1994) is a helpful source for this description.

The development of transport infrastructure systems in Sweden is contrasted by similar processes in other countries and at a supranational or federal level in the EU and the USA. Here, both historical and present comparisons are made. Bogart (2009), Chandler (1977, 1990), Clifton et al. (2011), and Millward (2005, 2011) are examples of valuable sources for some of these issues with regard to the US and European developments. Levinson (2002) and Roth (2006) provide valuable insights into many of the issues around private-sector engagement in the road sector in the UK and the USA.

Another comparison made to some extent is between transport infrastructure and other infrastructure systems such as telecommunication, energy/electricity, the financial sector, and postal services. These sectors have also been dominated by the government as owner or by different regulations. However, during the last 30 years a change in ownership, regulation, and geographical scope has altered the organization and development of these sectors in the direction of deregulation and liberalization. The current debate in many countries following the financial crisis has been going in the direction of questioning some of the deregulation decisions taken in more recent decades. Government involvement and regulation is clearly something that shifts over time.

In a recent report, Ottosson and Andersson-Skog (2013) provided an overview of regulation policies in a broad set of infrastructure sectors in Sweden. This is a good complement to the analysis here in many ways. Alexandersson (2010) has described the deregulation of bus and railway sectors in Sweden in the last decades, which gives an interesting parallel to the discussion around the government's role and its policy formation. The development over time of the road and railroad systems and the government's role is discussed with a basis in a coevolutionary approach. According to this approach, the development can be interpreted and understood as being influenced by technology, economics/organizational aspects, and by politics/socio-culture. The hypothesis is that these factors have influenced the development over time to a varying extent and led the government to have different views with regard to whether to provide transport infrastructure as part of the public or private sector.

The international comparisons of strategic transport infrastructure planning are guided both by economic theory, theory around planning in general, and more specifically urban/spatial planning. The situations faced in different countries while planning for infrastructure and the approaches taken when it comes to financing and ownership of transport infrastructure are analyzed with the use of theories about how coordination can be achieved. The discussion is widened through the application of aspects from classical liberal economic theory and political economy.

The interviews have been carried out with senior officials, politicians, and experts/scholars. These have been centered round a number of themes covering the historical development of the government's role over time, the use of cost–benefit analysis, and other welfare economics-based methods for prioritization and analysis. The current and future development in the EU and the US transport infrastructure policy and the future challenges of the government's role have been further themes for discussion in these interviews. The interviews are used as a general background to the analysis and descriptions and have not been used for explicit references.

The large number of reorganizations that have taken place in many countries, especially in the railroad sector, makes comparisons of organizational structures and their efficiency between countries difficult. Comparisons of productivity and cost-efficiency of transport infrastructure systems are published from time to time in both a European context and US context. In general, however, conclusions are difficult to draw when the organizational aspects are taken into consideration.

Short and Kopp (2005) have made similar observations with regard to cross-country studies throughout the member countries in of the Organization for Economic Co-operation and Development (OECD) in relation to infrastructure planning. A cross-country discussion on the efficiency of transport infrastructure systems can, however, be found in a report from the OECD/International Transport Forum (2008).

In 2009, Merkert published a quantitative analysis that focused on transaction costs in the railroad sector wherein the transaction costs of the British, German, and Swedish railroad systems are compared in specific with a view on reorganization and contracting out. The conclusion is that transaction costs are measurable but that they seem to be lower than anticipated with reference to the discussion on these topics. This is an ambitious piece of research showing the potential of quantitative approaches. However, it does not take the more general institutional or political settings in the different countries into consideration.

As previously mentioned, Millward and others have presented cross-country studies exemplifying the development of public and private enterprise in different infrastructure sectors, which gives a broad overview of many of the comparative perspectives. The organizational and institutional aspects of the government's role, which are among the primary focus areas here, are often difficult to capture in a quantitative analysis, partly since they deal with the qualitative realm to a higher degree than the quantitative. There are, however, a number of possible extensions of the analysis into the quantitative field.

The historical background and the description of the development over time of transport infrastructure systems and of the government's role in Chapter 5 are based primarily on official government and parliamentary documents from different time periods. Whether there is a connection between government decisions and actual measures implemented and carried out can of course be questioned. There are a number of possible difficulties connected to this view as detailed in, for example, public choice theories. One thing is that the government in practice might not actually have supported exactly those aims of transport infrastructure policy stated in the proposals. One reason might be that the government does not reveal its full or final bargaining position in order not to weaken its bargaining position in the early stages of the negotiation process around nationalization with the private railroad corporations in the 1930s.

Moreover, the government agencies might, in line with many studies of the functioning of the public sector, not have wanted to act in line with the government's decisions. This can be seen a number of times throughout the history of transport infrastructure policy, as the transport agencies and single actors for example in Sweden seem to have continued following previous transport policy decisions rather than more recent decisions.

2.1.2 The Research Process behind this Book

The research project leading to this book was part of my PhD-project during 2010 and 2013 (Hasselgren 2013a). The project started out as a planning and decision-analysis PhD program but became gradually more and more focused on economic theory and the evolving history of economic thought. Other research areas that were included in my studies were industrial economics, political science/sociology, and institutional theory for the economic and social sciences.

A major part of the reading focused on texts discussing the divide between public and private orderings in society and the concepts of government failure and market failure. As part of the research project papers and reports were published reflecting on international aspects and comparisons of transport infrastructure systems. A first paper was published as an annex in the report on transport infrastructure co-financing, which was presented by a Swedish government committee in 2011 (SOU 2011:49). A report was presented in 2012 and published by the Chamber of Commerce in Stockholm, Sweden (Hasselgren 2012). This report focuses on the historical development of the government's role, current development in a number of countries in the field of financing, and organization of transport infrastructure management. Finally, a number of suggestions for reform of the Swedish transport infrastructure sector were presented.

In April 2011, an article outlining some of the basic concepts of the research project was published in *Ekonomisk Debatt*, the journal of the Swedish Economic Association (*Nationalekonomiska föreningen*) (Hasselgren 2011a). In May 2011, at a research conference arranged by Södertörn University College and the Stockholm Institute of Transition Economies, a similar article was presented on privatization and liberalization focusing on network industries and Eastern Europe (Hasselgren 2012).

Another integral part of the research project has been the preparation of a report to the government's Expert Group for Public Economics (ESO) during 2012–2013 (Hasselgren 2013c). It covers the historical development of transport infrastructure financing and organization based on the coevolutionary model, which is also a basic view here. The ESO report also includes an international overview of current developments in six other countries and at the European Union level.

In parallel to the research project, a report (Hasselgren 2013b) focusing the goods transportation market and the prospects for increasing efficiency in the transport infrastructure systems supporting these services was studied in a report for the Transport Group (*TransportGruppen*, an umbrella organization for associations and companies in the transportation sector in Sweden).

Furthermore, a number of presentations have been given with regard to the research project in the Ministry of Enterprise's Transport Policy Department, the Swedish Transport Administration, Transport Analysis (the Swedish agency for analysis of transport policy), and at the annual Swedish Transport Research Conference (2011, 2012, and 2013), which is arranged by the Swedish National Road and Transport Research Institute (VTI). Presentations in relation to the research project have also been given in a number of other major Swedish transport-related conferences and seminars, for example, the First Swedish National Conference on Transport Research held in 2012.

A background paper was presented at the US Transportation Research Board's Annual Meeting in Washington, DC in January 2012 (Hasselgren 2011b). A revised version of that article was published in the *Scandinavian Journal of Public Administration* (Hasselgren 2013a). The article discusses the decision process around the nationalization of roads and railroads in the 1930–1940s and the arguments used in the debate leading to the nationalization. The strength and influence on the development of different arguments are also discussed. The following development of the government's ownership role is analyzed using the coevolutionary approach, which is presented in Chapter 3.

2.2 Some Perspectives on Transport Infrastructure

2.2.1 The Transport System—Functions and Temporal Perspectives

When analyzing the transport infrastructure system, it is helpful to make a distinction between:

- the physical transport infrastructure systems, represented by assets, here mainly roads and railroads; and
- the functional use of the transport infrastructure systems for carrying out transports services.

It is of course reasonable to question whether the two concepts can be separated in a meaningful way from an economic point of view. Roads and railroads, as physical assets, have a market value or book value that can be traced back to the cost of construction less depreciation plus the remaining value of reinvestments and maintenance. Without actual transport services being carried out on the physical network, the economic value of roads and railroads is rather the net value of the physical assets such as rail (iron), signaling cables (copper), and sand and rock-filling in road and rail embankments.

Lately, due to high prices of iron and copper, some theft of rails and cables have been reported by the Transport Administration in Sweden, signaling the existence of such a basic residual value. Normally, one could expect the physical assets to have few alternative uses. The market value of the physical assets in a situation without any transport services carried out is therefore generally limited. Following this reasoning the normal thing could be to expect the infrastructure and transportation to be seen as one combined functional system. This would also be an argument for vertical integration, with both transport operations and infrastructure management in the same organization, such as the way classic railroad corporations in Europe used to be organized and many railroad organizations are still organized.

However, analyzing the transport and transport infrastructure sector, we find that the opposite is often the case—that is disintegration. Historical incumbent railroad agencies have been disintegrated in many countries. Airports and harbors are other examples of infrastructure assets that are often organized as separate entities from transport services in the respective sectors. Electricity networks are also to some extent organized separately from electricity corporations. Networks for telecommunications and data transmission (in a wide meaning) are other examples of separately provided infrastructure systems, as are platforms and infrastructure for securities trading in the financial sector, for example.

Road systems have not been integrated like railroads. This is due to the fact that road systems are open, which makes traffic planning unnecessary, except for in congested areas or in the relatively rare situations when technical standards like bridge capacity constitute barriers that make planning necessary. For railroads, which is a closed system, capacity planning is crucial for safety and optimization of capacity utility. The need for capacity planning and rationing could be one of the reasons that makes integration between infrastructure and transport services justified.

The business of and risks connected to organizing and managing transport infrastructure systems are often drastically different from those of transport services. While transport infrastructure has a long-term perspective, transport services are generally more short-term oriented and more directly influenced by short-term relative price changes. Every single transport customer and transport can be seen as new in this perspective, while roads and railroads are rather stable systems. The business risks connected to transport infrastructure have more to do with fairly slow changing patterns of travel and transportation demand, connected to the regional development at large.

Over time, there have been numerous examples where it has been possible to implement systems where the users must pay for the use of transport infrastructure systems. There are examples where such systems have been in use for a long time. Toll road financing existed in the nineteenth century (Levinson 2002) and railroads also have to a large extent been financed through direct user fees from the outset. The development of technology to enable payments as, GSM-based tolling systems, which has further separated transport services and the transport infrastructure system, has created an argument for transport infrastructure as a separate system more and more realistic and important. This possible separation between infrastructure and transport services, though based on the understanding that there are close connections between the physical and functional system, is one of the backdrops and inspirations of my interest for the subject at large.

The transport system can also be discussed and managed with a focus on different time perspectives. In the short run, the main focus is to manage the current system with as limited resources as possible at any given service level and outreach of the system. Since roads and railroads are primarily managed by government agencies in Sweden, the revenue focus in the operations is often limited, which would be a prioritized focus area for a private corporation managing these systems.

In the medium term, allocation of resources for maintenance and reinvestment, which is a major task when it comes to roads and railroads, is the focus. Here, the perspective is often influenced by both allocative and distributive/regional aspects, more so than in the short run. The geographical allocation of scarce resources and whether allocation should follow some regional redistributive policy or focus on adaptation to transport volume is generally one balancing point in these considerations.

In the long term, the development of the road and railroad systems has to do with extensions to the systems, while roads and railroads are less frequently taken out of use. With this time perspective, and also to some extent in the short and medium term, cost–benefit analysis, a tool based on welfare economics and equilibrium style analysis, is in widespread use. The internal and external effects related to the transport system (both infrastructure and projected transport flows) are estimated and cost measures and revenues, or cost reductions are calculated. The net of these social costs and revenues are compared to the construction cost, discounted to present value, and a net present quote is the outcome of the calculation. Today, this method is the dominating tool to base decisions on allocation of resources for new construction and reinvestment in roads and railroads in most countries.

2.2.2 Functional Roles and Spatial Dimensions

Transport infrastructure systems can be analyzed both from a functional perspective as systems with varying scope and from a spatial dimension. The functional perspective entails roles such as financing, ownership, and regulation, while the spatial dimension represents the different levels of government. There are normally public-sector entities at a national, regional, and local level in most countries. The division of responsibility between these levels differs according to historical reasons and the degree of centralization in different countries.

In the case of Sweden, there is a mix between fairly nation-state-oriented policy settings, with a long-standing tradition of independent local governments. There is also a formally independent regional level in Sweden. Both the local and regional levels have the right to raise income tax independently from the government, but within financial limits set in specific legislation. Transport infrastructure is divided between the central, regional, and local levels in the public administration, though with a relatively large national road system compared to many other countries.

Governments in most countries have over time taken on a role that is complex, since it includes many roles both at a horizontal (functional) and vertical (spatial) level. This can be displayed in a schematic figure, see Fig. 2.1.

The government thus acts as financer, regulator, manager, and owner of the transport infrastructure system. Financing has to do with raising funds for the financing of the systems but also with the amortization or depreciation of the assets' value. Regulation entails both the legal system and setting in general, and when it comes to areas such as competition regulation and transport-related legislation and regulation. Management

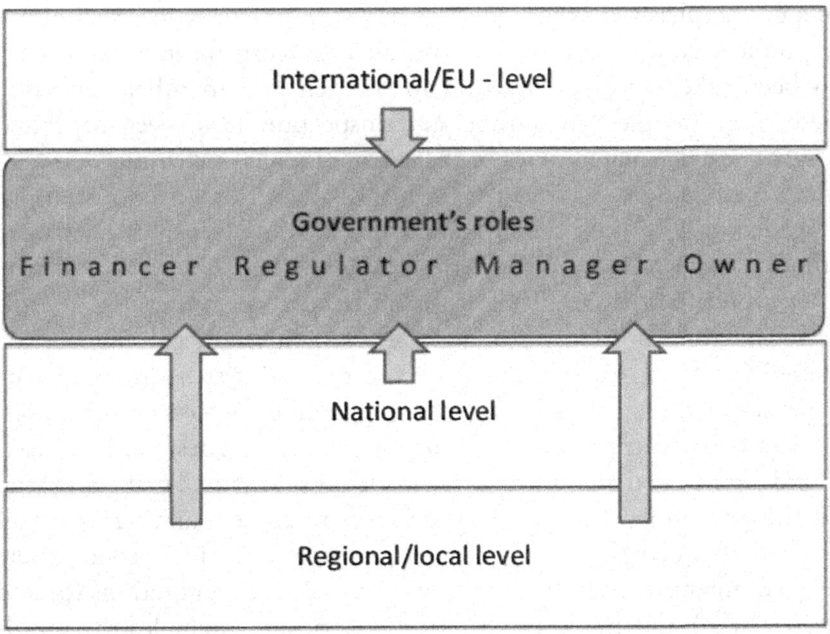

Fig. 2.1 Government's functional roles in transport infrastructure and different spatial levels

of the system is generally carried out through the transport agencies but can also be organized through the ownership of corporations or public utilities.

Furthermore, the government is active at the international, national, and regional/local levels in the system. The government thus is influenced by and must collaborate with actors in a spatial setting where actors at the international, national, and regional/local levels have direct access to the government. It could perhaps be argued that the collaboration is particularly dynamic in this sector since the actors at the other levels have such important and independent roles and mandates. Therefore, the government is involved in a vast number of projects and collaborative situations where management skills and decisiveness are important. The cross section of functional roles and spatial levels results in a number of possible roles and role conflicts between the different roles and goals at the different levels in the system.

To separate roles that might come into conflict is something that is generally emphasized when good governance practices for example in the public sector are discussed. A number of reorganization steps have also been taken in that direction in Sweden and in other countries, where, for example, supervision and inspection have been separated from the operational agencies in the sector. This has taken place in relation to the decision to merge the former Road and Rail Administrations in Sweden in 2009, and the formation of a separate transport regulatory authority, the Transport Agency (Bill 2008/09:31).

Another potential conflict lies in the resource planning and coordinating functions of the government agencies, especially for railroads. As competition has been introduced in the railroad system for both passenger transport and freight transport, a number of new prioritization conflicts become apparent, as the new operators' requests for availability and capacity in the railroad network must be mediated. It is vital that the government, as long as it controls resource planning, treats all operators in a neutral way. Of course, a situation like in Sweden, where the government owns both the major rail transport corporations (SJ and Green Cargo) and the Transport Administration, might lead to suspicions from non-government actors that the neutrality of the resource planning is not upheld.

The present situation also makes the government's role complicated with regard to the different levels in the system. The growing importance of transport policy at the EU level makes it necessary for the government to focus more on these issues and to formulate national transport infrastructure strategies. These are necessary both in order to compete with other member states for resources and in order to influence the policy development in the EU in a way that is favorable for Sweden.

Growing powers of regions and local governments in many countries make the government's presently fairly active role at these levels ambiguous, for example when it comes to the government's role in urban regeneration in relation to rail and road projects in cities. Should the government act as a provider of a functional system focusing on the system's internal efficiency, or should wider social aspects be included in the role? A widening of the government's role in these situations has been a dominant theme during the last few decades. A number of related issues, both at the national and supranational levels, are discussed in the theoretical field named "multi-level governance," see Peters and Pierre (2004).

In these cases, the government administrations might become involved as commercial counterparts to local governments and other actors, and as system providers. In many other sectors in Sweden and elsewhere, the government has chosen to leave similar active roles at the regional and local levels in favor of evaluator and supervisor roles. This is true for national general spatial planning and the public education system (excluding universities), which was transferred to the local governments in the 1990s. In other areas, the government has recently strived for stronger inspection and evaluation of local government's activities. This could be seen as a sign of the government's reregulation.

Most of the former government-owned public utilities in sectors like energy, telecommunication, and transport, of which today a majority have been transformed to corporate structures, also had objectives set by the government for their regional and local operations. Today, these are mostly transformed to corporations where the government does not generally control the day-to-day operations of the businesses but influences some of the services by inspection or regulation. One of the main reasons for this change has been the view that the government should stay out of situations where goal conflicts of this kind might evolve, based on a subsidiarity view also expressed in Sweden's constitution act (*Regeringsformen*) (1974: 152). The transport infrastructure system still entails a number of complexities that have been reduced in many other sectors in the economy.

References

Alexandersson, G. (2010). *The Accidental Deregulation: Essays on Reforms in the Swedish Bus and Railway Industries 1979–2009* (Doctoral Dissertation, Stockholm School of Economics).

Alvfors, K.-G. (1977). *Järnvägsförstatligandet - svensk järnvägspolitik under 1930-talet*, Svenska järnvägsklubbens skriftserie nr 21.

Andersson-Skog, L. (1993). *Såsom allmänna inrättningar till gagnet, men affärsföretag till namnet. SJ, järnvägspolitiken och den ekonomiska omvandlingen efter 1920*, Aa Umeå.

Bill 2008/09:31 Transportstyrelsen och dess verksamhet, Stockholm.

Blomkvist, P. (2001). *Den goda vägens vänner – Väg- och billobbyn och framväxten av det svenska bilsamhället 1914–1959*. Stockholm/Stehag: Brutus Östlings Bokförlag Symposion.

Bogart, D. (2009). Nationalizations and the Development of Transport Systems: Cross-Country Evidence from Railroad Networks, 1860–1912. *The Journal of Economic History, 69*(1), 202–237.

Chandler, A. D. (1977). *The Visible Hand: The Managerial Revolution in American Business*. Cambridge, MA, USA: The Belknap Press of Harvard University Press.

Chandler, A. D. (1990). *Scale and Scope: The Dynamics of Industrial Capitalism*. Cambridge, MA, USA: The Belknap Press of Harvard University Press.

Clifton, J., Lanthier, P., & Schröter, H. (2011). Regulating and Deregulating the Public Utilities 1830–2010. *Business History, 53*(5), 659–672.

Hasselgren, B. (2011a). En mer effektiv transportinfrastruktur. *Ekonomisk Debatt, 39*(6), 20–34.

Hasselgren, B. (2011b). *The Reluctant Infrastructure Manager: Nationalization of Rail and Road Infrastructure in Sweden, 1930 to 1940*. Presented at Transportation Research Board's Annual Meeting 2012, USA.

Hasselgren, B. (2012). *Effektivare transportinfrastruktur – med ny organization och finansiering*. Rapport för Stockholms Handelskammare 2012:1, Stockholm.

Hasselgren, B. (2013a). *Government's Role for Transport Infrastructure—Theoretical Approaches and Historical Development.* (PhD Dissertation, KTH Royal Insititute of Technolgy, Stockholm).

Hasselgren, B. (2013b). *Näringslivets transporter, Hur kan transportinfrastrukturen bli mer effektiv?* Research Report for the Transport Group (*TransportGruppen*), ISSN 1653-6126, Stockholm.

Hasselgren, B. (2013c). *Transportinfrastrukturen i förändring, Organisering och finansiering.* ESO-rapport, juni 2013, Finansdepartementet, Stockholm.

Kaijser, A. (1994). *I fädrens spår....* Stockholm: Carlssons Bokförlag.

Levinson, D. M. (2002). *Financing Transportation Networks.* Cheltenham: Edward Elgar.

Merkert, R. (2009). *The Organization of European Railways: A Transaction Cost Perspective.* The University of Leeds, Institute for Transport Studies.

Millward, R. (2005). *Private and Public Enterprise in Europe.* UK: Cambridge University Press.

Millward, R. (2011). Public Enterprise in the Modern Western World: An Historical Analysis. *Annals of Public and Cooperative Economics, 82*(4): 378–398.

OECD/International Transport Forum (ITF). (2008). *Transport Infrastructure Investment: Options for Efficiency.* Paris: OECD.

Ottosson, J. (1997). Path Dependence and Institutional Evolution: The Case of the Nationalisation of Private Railroads in Interwar Sweden. In L. Magnusson & J. Ottosson (Eds.), *Evolutionary Economics and Path Dependence* (pp. 186–196). Cheltenham: Edward Elgar.

Ottosson, J., & Andersson-Skog, L. (2013). *Stat, marknad och reglering i historiskt perspektiv.* Uppdragsforskningsrapport 2013:3. Swedish Competition Authority (*Konkurrensverket*), Stockholm.

Peters, B. G., & Pierre, J. (2004). Multi-Level Governance and Democracy: A Faustian Bargain? In I. Bache & M. Flinders (Eds.), *Multi-Level Governance.* Oxford: Oxford University Press.

Roth, G. (Ed.). (2006). *Street Smart, Competition, Entrepreneurship and the Future of Roads.* The Independent Institute, Transaction Publishers.

Short, J., & Kopp, A. (2005). Transport Infrastructure: Investment and Planning. Policy and Research Aspects. *Transport Policy, 12*(4): 360–367.

SOU 2011:49 Medfinansiering av transportinfrastruktur, Stockholm.

The Instrument of Government (*Regeringsformen*), 1974:152.

3

Economic Theory and Transport Infrastructure

3.1 Introduction

In this chapter, the theoretical paradigms as introduced in Chapter 2, as well as a coevolutionary approach, are described in greater detail. A stationary, or equilibrium-oriented, view has been contrasted against a more dynamic or emergent view on the economy and societal processes. It should be noted that the dichotomy between the neoclassical paradigm and the institutional paradigm presented earlier is outlined here with the perspectives sketched as ideal types more than representations of the actual current standing in each of the two paradigms, where these to some extent tend to blend in practical applications. It could be argued that analysis based on neoclassical theory is also open to the existence of less than perfect information and bounded rationality. And equilibrium-oriented analysis is often applicable when organizations, rather than social or welfare economics guided allocation, are the focus of the analysis.

Milgrom and Roberts (1992) and Laffont and Tirole (1993) are examples of scholars who have applied more formal models to organizational and incentive-centered problems. Williamson is a scholar whose

B. Hasselgren, *Transport Infrastructure in Time, Scope and Scale*,
https://doi.org/10.1007/978-3-319-79054-1_3

analysis, though framed within the institutional paradigm, sometimes comes close to neoclassical style theorizing. In many of Williamson's analyses, economizing behavior in a more stable environment is the basis of the organizational approach and conclusions.

The discussion concerning the two dominating theoretical paradigms in this book is to a large extent based on the theoretical discussion in academia at about the same time as many of the studied processes actually took place. The nationalization of roads and railroads during the 1930–1940s is an example that was discussed partly in relation to the theoretical discussion at that time. It is also apparent that new economic theories were generated in relation to the introduction and growth of railroads and roads in the late nineteenth and mid-twentieth centuries, respectively. Transport infrastructure related problems often generated a need for new theorizing.

Figure 3.1 summarizes some of the core elements in relation to the view on goals, organizations, actors, information, and so on in the two paradigms under primary discussion here.

Even if tendencies for synthesis are apparent, one strand of economic theory is clearly leaning toward a neoclassical view, where optimization and formal description in microeconomics mathematical models are more at the forefront. Another strand in economic theory where organizations and a broader set of factors in society (such as the wider institutional framework) are focused more than formal theories, and equilibrium analysis is represented by the institutional paradigm.

This divide when discussing the economy and societal processes is described by Wagner (2007) as two realms where people live. Wagner argues that there is often a tendency to overemphasize the welfare economics aspects on the functioning of the economy underestimating the dynamic and emerging aspects of public policy and the government's functioning. According to Wagner, since most people live in multiple and evolving public spheres, such as the market and the public sector, the Pareto efficient stable state analysis found in neoclassical welfare economics would generally not suffice as analytical tool. More often than the opposite we live in entangled realities where public and private sector spheres interact, negotiate, and are involved in exchange.

Feature	Neoclassical paradigm	Institutional paradigm
Overriding goal	Optimized outcome	Satisfactory outcome
Actors' goals	Individual utility maximizers with given and stable preferences.	Individually maximizing individual goals and learning over time with different preferences as a starting point and result.
Information	Perfect information. Objective	Bounded and limited information. Subjective
Role of prices	Transfers information on the resource use in the economy based on a utility view.	Transfers information on production and transaction costs as a basis for decisions and learning.
Transaction costs	Negligible	Important for understanding how the economy and market functions. Varying over time and between markets.
Organizational view	Non-reflected view or seen as unimportant and/or rational view.	Organizations a tool for handling transaction costs. Critical view on the rationality of organizations.
Government intervention	Rational view. Government intervention as a tool for adjusting market imperfections.	Bounded rationality. Government action problematic either for a rent-seeking behavior, lack of representation, or since markets are seen as better tools for learning and evolution than government organization.

Fig. 3.1 Neoclassical and institutional theories—some features (*Source* Based on Klein (1998) and Huerta de Soto (2010))

The view that intentionality and personal/private aims often affect decision processes, such as in the case of theories of entrepreneurship and innovation, principal/agency theory or in relation to contract/transaction cost theory, is besides the neoclassical/institutional divide, an important part of the theoretical approach here. This self-interested behavior model has been the starting point for many theories around societal processes and individual behavior. In the discussion around the scientific approach, literature such as Hernes (2008), which presents a number of views on organizations and change "in a tangled world," entails a number of helpful sources with regard to the relation between individual actors and organizations. Medema (2009) describes the evolution over time of theories connected to the view on self-interest and its relation to societal interests. Processes which can be seen as individually maximizing are often in the end through social interaction also socially maximizing or at least pleasing.

Public choice theorizing, in accordance with scholars like Buchanan and Tullock (1962), has been focused on understanding the functioning of political systems based on a view with individually maximizing actors in and outside the political system, as well as in bureaucracies as the core model. Public choice theorizing is one useful tool when analyzing important areas in governments' activities like transport infrastructure. This is true both for discussions around decision-making concerning resource allocation in general and issues related to financing. The balance between fee models and tax-based systems, with or without earmarking specific areas, is one such question that is discussed by Wagner (1991/2011).

Another theoretical area that lies at the heart of this analysis is *planning theory* and the view on planning and coordination in general. For the government to be a better owner and manager of transport infrastructure than lower levels in the public sector or market actors, there must be a belief that sectors like transport infrastructure must be managed and controlled at higher and central levels in the system. For this to be possible, the central planning level must have the means and capacity to collect and make use of information and knowledge about the system, the needs of users, and the appropriate measures to take.

Here, the rationally functioning ideal government model is contrasted against a likewise perhaps idealistic view on the market's ability to achieve spontaneous ordering in many systems. Hayek (1944) provided a classical basis for a critical view on government-led planning in his book *Road to Serfdom*, which has been one inspiration for the view on planning here. Hayek criticized government planning based on Second World War experiences and with references to Marxist-inspired Soviet Union style planning systems.

Schumpeter (1942, 1950) gave a similar concerned picture on the future of the capitalistic system, but with a view that the "march into socialism" (p. 415) was more or less inevitable as a result of the strong driving forces for large-scale production and loss of individual and personal ownership in the centralized structures connected to modern capitalism.

Examples in the same tradition, where a critical classic liberal approach to government intervention is followed, can be found in Pennington (2011) and Klein (2012), both with examples from transport infrastructure and land use planning. Pennington (2004) has also discussed the balance between communicative planning methods, as inspired by Habermas, and market-based systems, exemplifying the pros and cons of the two perspectives with a preference for the market model. A well-developed defense for communicative, or critical planning theory, has been presented recently by Sager (2012). Sager argues that communicative-based planning methods are, without question, superior to the neoliberal planning view, as he prefers to name market-based models.

Another angle in the literature connected to the neoclassical versus institutional divide is the tradition discussing *the balance between market organization and government intervention*. The broad historical perspectives in the thinking around self-interest and the public interest are outlined by Medema (2009). Medema argues that a discussion on the perceived need to limit the force of self-interest is traceable at least back to the ancient Greek philosophers. The general view, according to Medema, has been that self-interest must be limited in order to achieve a good societal outcome. Primarily through the thinking of Adam Smith and a number of later scholars in the classical liberal tradition has the pursuit of self-interest been seen as consistent with a pleasing overall outcome for society.

More specific discussions directly related to transport infrastructure and government handling of the provision of public goods based on regulation can be found in Coase's articles from the late 1940s (1946, 1947) around the financing principles primarily for roads and railroads and the 1960 article The Problem of Social Cost. These will be further discussed in Chapter 5.

The combined message in this literature is that there has been a long-standing discussion on the balance between market and government and the individual interest in relation to the public interest. All of the scholars mentioned above in the liberal tradition strive for an understanding of the effects individuals' limited perception might have on the prospects of planning and government intervention. Scholars in the neoclassical tradition tend to take the failure of individual action more or less for granted thus motivating government intervention in order to increase efficiency. This is generally the case in transport infrastructure related analysis, where market failure is generally the starting point of the discussion rather than an analytical outcome based on empirical observation (Fig. 3.2).

Another theoretical area of interest is of course *public finance* with its theorizing around fiscal practices of the public sector. Gruber (2011) is a good example from this theoretical field, providing a number of analyses from different sectors. In public finance, the view on the government as an entity that has the right, and should, to act in order to overcome deficient market practices or outcomes is often contrasted against views where the influence of public intervention should be limited through, for example, claims on the relevance of "Wicksellian" decision rules such as absolute majority voting rules as guides for tax policy (Blankart and Fasten 2011). The government can within a public finance view either be seen as a unified hierarchical organization

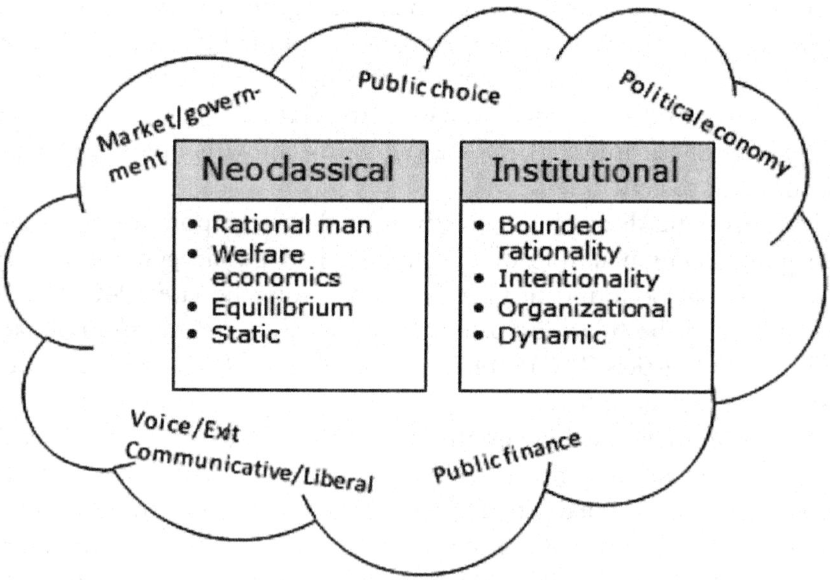

Fig. 3.2 Core theoretical approaches and additional approaches

that influences the surrounding economy to achieve specified goals or, alternatively, as a process or flow where different interests compete in a polycentric process to attract influence and power over different processes. In this latter form, the government is less clear as a distinct actor in the economy (Wagner 2007). While scholars like Gruber can justify intervention by offering concise action, proposals to alleviate deficiencies others, like Wagner, tend to hesitate in giving clear advice since the outcome of social processes is in general unclear.

A summary of the theoretical approaches is presented in Fig. 3.3. The two main paradigms at the core and some of the more practical applications of these in transport infrastructure such as financing principles are presented. It is argued that the two central paradigms here and their applications have influenced the historical development of

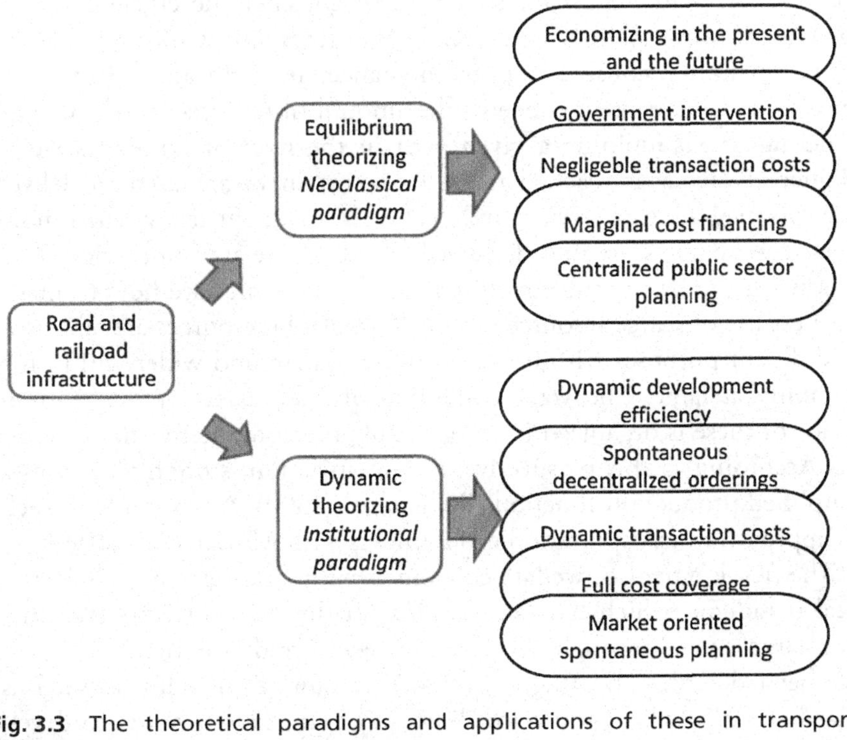

Fig. 3.3 The theoretical paradigms and applications of these in transport infrastructure

the government's role in transport infrastructure. These are more or less eternal questions related to major societal systems and organizations. We will find both of the paradigms and their applications in most sectors and that they still affect the current discussions. And the balancing between the perspectives is part of the management of transport infrastructure systems.

3.2 Neoclassical Theories and Welfare Economics

3.2.1 Natural Monopoly Theory

Transport infrastructure systems represent major physical assets with a considerable value. This makes it vital to consider the efficient use of these assets through good management routines and working processes for the planning, construction, maintenance, and utilization. Efficiency measured in this respect concerns the amount of resources used for constructing or maintaining a given asset in the road or railroad system. Higher efficiency is reached when lesser resources are used to deliver any specified asset or service, and vice versa lower efficiency when more resources are necessary in order to achieve the same asset or service.

Among the basic problems discussed in economics are how to make the best use of scarce resources and how available resources are allocated to different purposes within the transport system and wider within the economy at large. The way production of fixed assets or the maintenance of these is organized is not generally the core interest in economics. According to this perspective, the organization is often viewed as a simplified production function (Williamson 2000). An example of such an approach in transportation economics is with McCarthy (2001).

The development of welfare economics with an origin in the neoclassical paradigm, which has been applied in the transport infrastructure to a large extent through the late nineteenth and twentieth centuries, has been described by Ruggles (1949). A number of scholars such as Marshall, Wicksell, Pigou, Hotelling, and Lerner contributed to developing a view where consumers' marginal utility in relation to different choices of goods and services should be the basis for the analysis of resource allocation in the economy. This also led to the development of a view where government intervention was seen as justified from a theoretical standpoint. Through the use of taxes or fees, or regulation, a resource utilization closer to an optimum should be achieved. Pigou was one of the scholars who developed this view.

Hotelling (1938) published a well-known article where this view was applied to transport infrastructure systems, arguing for government intervention and subsidies in order to alleviate market failures. Part of the same view is that decreasing-cost industries, such as roads and railroads, could be expected to be run as nationalized or regulated monopolies in order to avoid inefficiencies.

In these cases, only marginal costs should be charged for the use of the products or services. The unfinanced part of the costs, which are not covered by marginal cost pricing based revenues, should, according to the same line of reasoning, primarily be paid for by the government and funded by tax revenues.

Blaug (2007) describes the development of this line of reasoning as the starting point of the growth of the view (also named the second welfare theorem), that deficits resulting from marginal cost pricing, in transport infrastructure systems should be covered by lump-sum taxes, distorting consumption decisions as little as possible. Following such initial corrections of the distribution of wealth in the economy markets should in principle be left to function according to the ideal market economy model. This view is still today among the cornerstones of neoclassical thinking around transport infrastructure.

Closely connected to the view that only a few providers of systems like transport infrastructure are likely to prevail has been the theoretical assertion that transport infrastructure systems can normally be seen as natural monopolies. Mosca (2008) presents a historical background to the concept and the use of natural monopoly theories. J. S. Mill used the term in 1848, the French economist Walras applied it explicitly to railroad networks in the 1870s, and the late nineteenth-century economist R. T. Ely even named an article by using the phrase "Natural monopolies…" Marshall discussed the same concepts but proposed that they be discussed as indivisible industries rather than natural monopolies. A more recent and influential application was given by Samuelson in the 1950s. In his 1954 article on the pure theory of public expenditure, Samuelsson divided the economy between goods provided on markets and goods provided by the public sector. This theory was later developed by Buchanan (1968).

The general deficiencies of payment systems opening for free riders have been furthered as support for the idea that there are in fact goods, such as transport infrastructure, that are preferably, and will likely be, provided by the public sector. These ideas have been strengthened by the existence of economies of scale and scope in the systems (implying diminishing marginal costs and positive network effects). All of these factors have according to the same view made the introduction of markets for the provision of transport infrastructure less viable.

The difficulties in introducing fee systems have been part of the motivation for the existence of non-excludability of marginal users in transport infrastructure systems. This is to say that public goods are difficult or impossible to deliver only to separate or excludable customers. A large proportion of free riders are thus likely in these systems. Another feature is that one user does not necessarily exclude another user from using the road, a phenomenon which has been discussed under the term non-rivalrous. This phenomenon is generally true but less relevant in congested areas such as cities and for railroads, where there is often a conflict around access to the available capacity. The existence of external effects, which are difficult to price, has been another line of reasoning, arguing for the necessity to treat roads and railroads as something special in the economy, underpinning the natural monopoly view.

Even if the welfare economics view of natural monopolies has been influential and is often reasonable as a metaphor, it can at the same time be argued that natural monopolies are not stable over time and are challenged by technological developments, economics, and political changes. Technological development represents one of the challenges to the view that natural monopolies exist and for the government's current role in transport infrastructure. Over time, a situation with a stationary rather than a dynamic situation in the economy is fairly unrealistic.

3.2.2 A Dichotomy of Failure and Success

The dichotomy between public and private goods, and possible organizational models for the provision of these goods, are presented in Fig. 3.4. Public goods can, according to Samuelson and others, be expected to be provided by a private or public monopoly. Private goods might though be provided either in markets or by the public sector.

A voluminous discussion has been developed around the (possible) dichotomy between public and private goods, or in parallel the boundaries between government and private sectors of the economy. One objection toward this focus is that the dichotomy has shifted the attention away from concerns about institutional arrangements to concerns of general resource allocation. Furthermore, most empirical investigations show that the boxes in figures such as the one above are almost impossible to fill out without running into difficulties with definitions (Wagner 2007) . This can be seen as an example of a criticism that has focused on the perhaps oversimplified modeling in neoclassical economics with the economy split into different blocks: market and

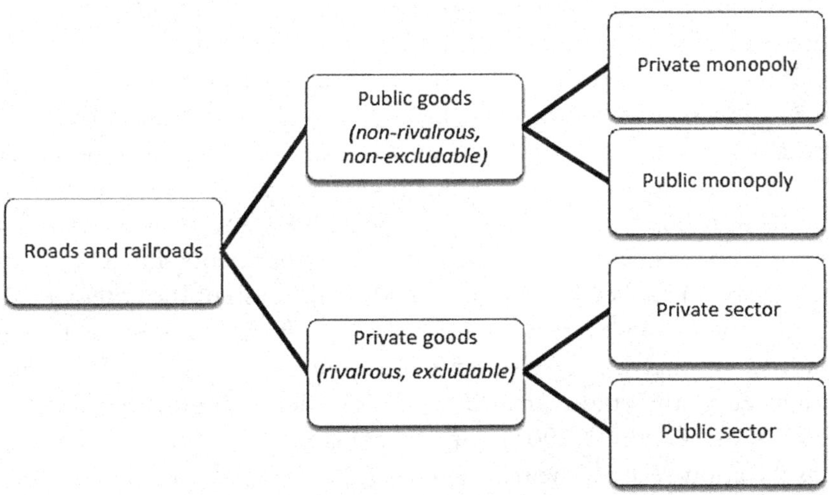

Fig. 3.4 Public and private goods and models for provision of these services and goods

non-market. In real life, there are examples of both the private provision of public goods and public-sector provision of private goods, which is exemplified in Fig. 3.4.

Connected to both public and private goods provision is the view that failures in relation to the provision of the goods and services might occur. Governments might fail both in the provision of private and public goods. Markets and private firms might in the same way fail when providing private or sometimes public goods.

3.2.3 Neoclassical Theory and Market Failure Views

Another aspect of the neoclassical theories is the discussion around what role the government should take and what role the market and individual actors should preferably have. Welfare economics-based theorizing, such as Pigovian arguments, focuses on achieving an optimal use of resources in the economy. By applying a yardstick, often Pareto criteria, redistribution of resources can be justified in order to arrive at a more optimal outcome. Market failures, however, also call for government intervention.

Intervention in order to rectify the spontaneous outcome of market processes can be implemented as regulations of the market to prohibit the use of technology with high emissions, to improve competition, enhance information sharing or through direct price adjustments through taxes, for example. Compensatory payments to groups that have been negatively affected by other parties' actions are a part of these possible government actions. Ruggles (1949) points to the unanimous advice by scholars like Samuelson and Arrow that such compensatory payments should be made "if an economic policy is to be advocated on the basis of the criteria established by the new welfare economics" (p. 39). Interventionism is thus in general connected to neoclassical welfare economics.

Analyzing the more recent transportation economics literature such as McCarthy (2001), it is apparent that the analysis of transportation-related themes based on microeconomics and welfare economics have been further developed along the line of the theories brought forward during the 1930–1940s. A number of classical microeconomic aspects on the producing firms in transportation, the demand functions, and markets operating under perfect competition or less than perfect conditions are discussed by McCarthy. Furthermore, the analytical dilemmas related to government regulation of transportation and infrastructure under different assumptions with regard to the market structure and the cost functions are analyzed. This also includes an analysis of investment decisions and issues such as congestion charging and concepts like first-best and second-best pricing of assets like transport infrastructure. In one chapter in McCarthy's (2001) textbook, the theoretical foundations and preconditions for a pricing and tax structure reflecting marginal costs for road charging, while also fulfilling a full cost financing requirement, are outlined. Under certain conditions such charging, in congested areas and primarily for roads, can cover the full costs of transport infrastructure.

Winston (1991) discusses efficient pricing rules for transport infrastructure investments from a marginal cost-based pricing system perspective, but adds that the government in general should add components to the marginal cost that include social cost elements, to give a correct price signal, for new investment. New capacity should be provided until the marginal benefit equals marginal costs. According to Winston, within such financing urban roads with capacity shortage should also meet the financing requirement. Rural roads would though need additional charges to "attain a balanced highway budget" (p. 120).

A common theme in this tradition since the 1930s, where McCarthy is a good example of theoretical accuracy, is the assumptions generally underpinning neoclassical theoretical work: perfect information, free entry and exit, perfect or constrained competition, and utility maximizing consumers with stable and comparable utility functions among different actors. The producing organizations are primarily seen as cost functions, following the maxims of profit maximization. Government intervention is justified whenever such intervention is seen, from a theoretical basis, to improve social welfare or an efficient resource allocation in the economy. The less than optimal functioning of the government and the public sector at large with less than perfect information as seen from a principal agent or political economy point of view is generally not reflected on.

Even if there are more dynamic decision problems, such as the choice between capital and labor or the market dynamics between competing transportation modes (also discussed by McCarthy), the more overarching dynamics in markets and the economy around entrepreneurship, innovation, and the functioning of the producing organizations are more or less left outside the discussion.

Another example of the neoclassical tradition is Parry and Bento (2001). They discuss the possible allocative efficiencies inherent in a theoretically interesting setting, where revenues from congestion charging could be used by the government in order to reduce taxes on labor. This would more than offset the negative supply effect connected to the introduction of congestion charges and, argues Parry and Bento, increases the efficiency of the user charge by more than 100%, while the congestion charge would still be equal to a Pigovian tax. This example also displays a limited interest in the government as a rather complicated actor and different public choice related problems. It comes close to what Coase has named "blackboard economics."

Newbery (1990) discusses congestion charging with the question of whether some kind of earmarking principles should be applied to the revenues from road charges in order to direct them to the "highway budget" (p. 2). Newbery argues that there is no "logical reason" for this, echoing insights from classical public finance theorizing. Earmarking might be a vital aspect of any organizational system in order to raise or achieve efficiency, as will be discussed below. A number of difficulties connected to implementing user charges in a public-sector setting are discussed by Wagner (1991/2011) from a classical public choice perspective, where user charges in public-sector setting might lead to suboptimal solutions.

Since the qualifications for an efficient equilibrium to result from spontaneous market activity according to the neoclassical model are difficult to meet, a large number of market failures are likely to be found, as has been exemplified above in the transportation policy literature. This opens for activism from the government's side. Pennington (2011) points to the fact that this view allows for a range of services "from the supply of public parks and lighthouses to the control of industrial pollution" to be "improved through targeted government action" (p. 20). A long history of government interventionism motivated by the believed inferior outcome of individual action and self-interest is also presented by Medema (2009). Beside ancient Greek philosophy and medieval scholasticism, Medema also traces the concern toward self-interest to liberals like Mill and socialists like Marx.

A parallel can also be found in the discussion on the origins of the accuracy of both marginal cost-based pricing and government intervention. The growth of large organizational units, such as those in transport infrastructure, is generally explained by the scale effects based on the introduction of new technology like railroads or capital-intensive machinery and production processes. Hayek (1944) and Schumpeter (1942) pointed to this development as an important sign of the development of the capitalist system of the twentieth century. Both of these remarks were made close to the time when transport infrastructure assets were about to be nationalized in many countries in Europe.

While Schumpeter described the growth of organizational size as a more or less inevitable process where nothing outside the "big concerns" (p. 142) will prevail, Hayek, however, discussed the growth of large-scale organizational units as a result of deliberate government action. Governments had participated in either shaping large units of organization through trade tariffs (USA) or protected the spontaneous cartels that private market actors had formed (Germany) (pp. 92–93). Thus, governments, by fostering larger organizational units in the economy, can be seen as underscoring the perceived need for more activist government policies, including marginal cost pricing. In this way, the importance of scale economies in transport infrastructure is exemplified both as an input to further political intervention and an outcome of intervention.

3.3 Institutional Theory and Organizational Focus

If neoclassical theory as applied to transport infrastructure focuses on finding optimal use of available resources and is open to government intervention in order to correct or improve the outcome of the market, institutional theory is more focused on the balance between market settings and organizations or hierarchies as a means of delivering and managing resources, taking into account transaction costs. The focus is, compared to neoclassics, to a higher extent set on development and dynamic processes, where organizational learning and the role of spontaneous activity in the economy is at the forefront. Emergent processes and learning are other concepts that are discussed in relation to this more dynamic approach. Nelson and Winter (1982) are among scholars who have introduced such evolutionary elements into theories around organization and learning. Some of the major contributions to a dynamic or evolutionary orientation of economics also came from scholars like Schumpeter, who introduced the creative destruction view but also theories of growth and business cycles during the early twentieth century.

Zappia (2001) describes the major efforts during the 1920–1940s by scholars like Lindahl and Hayek to understand and describe how neoclassical equilibrium analysis could be connected to dynamism and change. Zappia argues that Lindahl focused on how expectations are changed during development processes, while Hayek was more concerned with actors' behavior in different institutional settings, but also in a dynamic perspective. This might be seen as examples where the focus is set either on the individual actors, dynamic adaptation to change or alternatively on the institutional environment as such. Keeping his interest for dynamism and change in the economy, Hayek (1984) presented a view on economics and the economic system as ever-changing and dynamic Heraclitus based river-like metaphor, rather than stable and in equilibrium.

North (1990) and Ostrom (2005) have analyzed institutional development and factors influencing institutional growth in a historical perspective, and with regard to spontaneous decentralized orderings. A focus on values like ethics and moral sentiments as explanatory factors behind successful growth periods, rather than on formal institutions, is a central feature in some of the works of McCloskey. In her recent book *Bourgeois Dignity: Why Economics Can't Explain the Modern World* (2010), the tendency for a majority of the bourgeoisie to encompass values like the search for new knowledge and the creative-destructive power of that knowledge in transforming societies is brought to the forefront in understanding change and growth.

This latter view might be seen as pointing in the direction of different layers or aspects of factors that explain growth and change in societies. A model where different such levels of societal systems and their connection are displayed has been discussed by Williamson (2000). Four levels are included in the model presented by Williamson. These range from: (1) slowly changing cultural factors like customs and tradition; (2) the institutional environment, with judicial systems like property rights; (3) governance; and (4) most rapidly changing, resource allocation dilemmas facing most organizations, such as pricing and incentives. The model also entails interrelated loops between the different levels, pointing at the dynamism of the institutional perspective.

Institutional theory and its application in the transport policy sector have been discussed by Rietveld and Stough (2007). They point to the importance of property rights for the spread of road systems financed with tolling. Transaction costs connected to borders can explain why cross-border trade has been smaller in size than otherwise could have been expected. The size of trade and lack of economic integration between Sweden and Denmark in the Öresund region, as an example, have been discussed in these terms.

For the future, Rietveld and Stough single out institutional settings that support a development in line with claims for sustainability, the further regulatory reform to strengthen institutions that support efficiency, and the prospect for successful Public–Private Partnerships (PPP) projects as important. Rietveld (2012) has also later commented on cross-border aspects of transport from an institutional perspective.

Transaction cost theory is part of Williamson's model and an area that has been developed for analyzing the boundaries of organizations and the balance between markets and organizations/hierarchies. These theories can be applied to the transport infrastructure area to deepen the understanding of how and why different organization models are chosen. One such attempt has been presented by Hasselgren (2011). Mokyr (1990) discusses the importance of technological creativity and change in a development perspective. One of the themes in institutional theory has been the existence of transaction costs representing friction in the economic system, which can explain how and why different organizational solutions are chosen. Transaction costs can be analyzed in the short run as being stable, while in the long run are more flexible and dynamic. As mentioned above, Merkert (2009) presented a major analytical application of transaction cost theory to the railroad sector.

3.3.1 Stable and Dynamic Transaction Costs

For one of the purposes here, which is to analyze the balance between public and private sector provisions of transport infrastructure systems over time, transaction cost theory is one possible analytical tool. The transaction cost approach was introduced by Coase (1937) and developed by Williamson (1981). The original theories, which were developed for private sector organizations, have later been adopted for public-sector organizations by Williamson (1999) and further by Ruiter (2005).

The basic characteristics of transactions in Williamson's presentation are the asset specificity, uncertainty, and frequency of transactions. In relation to public-sector services, Williamson also introduced the attribute probity, which stands for the specific soft values of loyalty and rectitude common in some public-sector services. The characteristics of specific transactions can, according to Williamson, explain whether a complete contract can be made up and markets will prevail, or whether incomplete contracts will be the general situation and hierarchies, here possibly as part of the public sector, are more efficient. In circumstances when expected efficiencies of scale and scope, together with the incentives for more effective resource utilization originating from private ownership as compared to public-sector ownership, override deficiencies of private sector provision, the private sector/market model should be applied. This can be adjusted, according to Williamson, if the reasons for public-sector provision are strong enough. Risks of poor quality and high costs related to the administration of private monopolies, as one of the major deficiencies connected to private sector provision, naturally have to be considered in this discussion.

Figure 3.5 indicates that a number of the factors in the transport infrastructure sector seem to call for some kind of hierarchical solution to the organization of the systems. Assets in road and railroad systems are rather specific, there is generally a high degree of uncertainty around the construction and actual use of any single road or railroad section as it is completed. Road and railroad projects are often rather unique, which is why the learning related to construction and management can generally be expected to come closer to the "few" rather than the "many" characters in the figure. Furthermore, this calls for hierarchy rather than for market solutions. Though not clearly pointing in the direction of public-sector responsibility, the last of the aspects in Fig. 3.5, probity, might be the one that most clearly speaks in favor of market solutions. Neither in the construction or management phases of transport infrastructure systems might probity be seen as an important value, which should speak in favor of hierarchy and public-sector involvement. This is one of the aspects that does not speak in favor of necessary government intervention in transport infrastructure systems.

A more dynamic view on transaction costs has been forwarded by Langlois. An application of this view has been discussed by Langlois (2003), where diminishing transaction costs, in network industries, as studied by Chandler (1977, 1990) when it comes to railroads in the US railroad sector, are discussed in relation to the total output and thus wealth in an economy. As the total income level increases and transaction costs generally fall, the room for, or need for, managerial structures and hierarchical structures might diminish.

What interests Langlois (1992) is the process by which short-run transaction costs turn into long-run variable costs and the factors that explain this process. Langlois emphasizes learning that makes transaction cost to diminish. This learning occurs through the repeated

Aspect	Hierarchy	Market
Asset specificity	High	Low
Uncertainty	High	Low
Frequency	Few	Many
Probity	Important	Less important

Fig. 3.5 Transaction costs and cases for hierarchy or market organization (*Source* Williamson 1981, 1999)

transactions and evolution of norms of reciprocity and cooperation. The way the short and long run are connected is through the capabilities of the firm, which in turn is made up of skills, organization, and technology. Here, Langlois quotes Nelson and Winter (1982). On the one hand, firms are seen as pools of resources, and on the other hand, the importance of routines is the focus.

In the long-run, as transaction costs diminish, Langlois also argues that governance costs diminish, when relationships turn more and more routine-based. This would speak in favor of market solutions rather than hierarchies in the long run, since capabilities of the firm should be expected to diffuse into the market (Fig. 3.6).

This might imply a view wherein economies develop from pre-industrial invisible hand settings through industrialization's managerialist visible hand settings to post-industrialized vanishing hand settings. This third era would then represent a situation where transaction costs have become small in absolute terms and part of total output or wealth, which is also a parallel to the results in Merkert's (2009) analysis

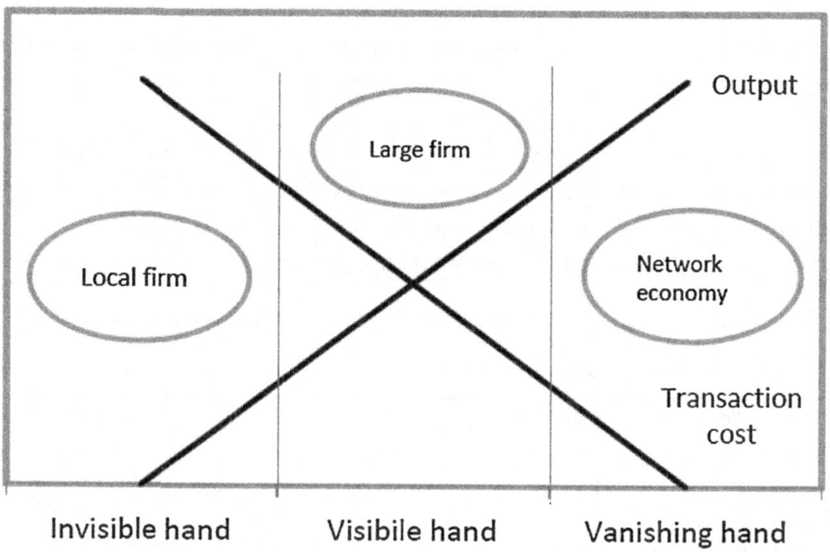

Fig. 3.6 Three areas of managerial practices and organisational forms over time (*Source* Based on Langlois (2003), adjusted)

of transaction costs in a number of railroad organizations in different countries. This might be why organization/hierarchy or management is no longer a crucial aspect of production systems. In this respect, the post-industrialization era's tendency for network-based production systems would call for less hierarchical systems and organizations. It could perhaps be argued that large-scale industries represent an earlier era in the industrial development, the value of which might be reduced in the future, while small-scale and network style systems might become more important.

3.3.2 Hybrid Organizations—The Middle Way?

Ruiter (2005) introduces hybrid forms between market and hierarchy to analyze transaction costs in public-sector settings, which seems appropriate to bring into the discussion. In one step of his analysis, Ruiter defines three different modes for the organization of public-sector governance:

- Full privatization
- Regulation
- Public agency

Out of the three models, the hybrid model with private actors, that supply goods and services to the public sector according to contracts, combined with public-sector functions in regulation and supervision is an example of a deregulation step taken in many other sectors (e.g., telecommunication). Since the government reasonably still will have important roles as regulator and financier, it seems less realistic to arrive at a situation where transport infrastructure could be provided solely on markets with full privatization. PPP in this respect might also represent one possible middle way between government and market.

Even if new financing and a new organizational setting called for a new organizational setup, the arguments in favor of large-scale organizations, which will allow for efficiencies of scale and scope, are still strong. A large-scale organization often leads to monopolistic tendencies, which makes regulation defendable in order to avoid monopolistic behavior. Perhaps the suggestion Langlois seems to make, in combination with Ruiter's assertion, points to possible future organizational models with fewer vertically integrated structures as transaction costs seem to become relatively less important. Public/private cooperation and smaller size rather than larger might be a way forward, if these theories should be followed.

3.4 A Coevolutionary Development Approach

The discussion and analysis here are concerned with the long-term development of transport infrastructure systems. An analysis like this is facilitated if it is guided by a theoretical approach that allows for understanding change over time and where a number of factors that influence the development are included. Since one focus area here is to explain and understand the balance between government and market provision of roads and railroads over time, this aspect is included in the approach as the outcome at every time during the development. Over time, transport infrastructure systems have been and are still organized in the private or in the public sector.

The coevolutionary perspective discussed here is related to a dynamic view on organizations. In this way, the coevolutionary perspective is connected to institutional theory. The evolution, even if not in biological terms, of organizations and firms over time is of course interesting to a broad historical overview and analysis like the one here.

A number of theories have been put forward to capture the evolution of societal systems such as transport infrastructure, where technology, economics, and institutions like political systems interact to shape the development. These factors are important in shaping institutional environments. The basic evolutionary concept goes back to discussions based on ecology in the 1960s, according to Bergh and Stagl (2003). A central point in this view is that coevolution has to do with the interaction between different kinds of systems/institutions. Nelson and Winter (1982) have provided an evolutionary perspective on economic change, which, as described earlier, is based on a dynamic view on the development of routines over time. Routines in specific organizations or firms determine, according to this view, what a firm does as a function of external variables and internal variables. Here is another example of a coevolutionary view.

Kaijser (2004) points to interesting aspects of the development of infrasystems, specifying them as socio-technical. Kaijser thus considers the institutional frameworks and the system culture, as well as technology. This reflects a coevolutionary stance with regard to development over time.

Following North's (1990) view on institutional change, both the organizations and the single actors or entrepreneurs in the organizations are active in shaping institutional change. North thereby focuses on the entrepreneur as an important agent in the development and change over time. Institutions, such as the economic and political systems, set the frameworks for the functioning and change of organizations and evolution of institutions. Important factors in this respect are the incentive systems and the transaction costs that are connected to different relations in organizations. Relative prices (and changes of relative prices) on markets are seen as driving forces for change, while change is seen to be continuous and incremental rather than revolutionary.

Tunzelmann (2003) connects technological change (or creation) with evolution of governance forms in organizations. This is described as a coevolutionary relation that is facilitated by relationships between technology and governance in the form of institutions, power relations, incentives, and knowledge bases. Tunzelmann argues that his model can be used to bring a deeper understanding of how market failures and/or government failures are related to the interdependencies of governance systems and technology. Transaction costs in different settings are discussed by North as an important factor to understand and explain institutional change. Transaction cost theory has been criticized from a number of angles, Leflavie (1996), is one example, to be too static, and not taking learning, agency, or power structures into account.

Here, Langlois (1992), as discussed above, offers a line of thinking that aims to adapt transaction cost theories with dynamism and evolution. The development of large corporations and industrial segments over time has been described and analyzed by Chandler (1992), who argues that evolutionary theory with its interest for organizational learning and the development of capabilities explains (better than transaction cost theory) how successful corporations and structures evolve. Chandler thereby emphasizes the importance of good management exemplified by knowledge, experience, and organizational design. Chandler also argues that such good management is at the core of the possibilities to reap efficiencies of scale and scope such as in large infrastructure systems, and why an evolutionary perspective is central.

A number of scholars have discussed the growth of public enterprises and public utilities, and the balance between public-sector activities and private sector alternatives in Western countries. Many of these have been studying transport infrastructure systems. A broad exposé over the growth of public and private enterprise in Europe has been provided by Millward (2005), showing a large variety of development patterns in different countries, but over time within a framework of gradual shifts between public and private ownership and management. Reasons for the choice of different organizational models and ownership in these sectors have been discussed by Clifton et al. (2011), who focused on regulation and deregulation patterns with regard to public utilities between 1830 and 2010, and by Millward (2011).

Bogart (2009) has analyzed railroad nationalization in a large number of countries focusing on reasons for nationalization but also differentiating countries according to legal traditions, for example. Andersson-Skog (1993) and Ottosson (1997) are working with a similar institutional model when discussing the organization of railroads in Sweden. In these latter examples, development is analyzed as dependent on economic factors such as natural monopoly tendencies, but also on political aspirations such as regional policy and distributive policies in general to be pursued through the management and ownership or regulation of utilities, for example. Bogart and Clifton et al. also point to the importance of military considerations for the governments' decisions on these matters. Here, the access to communication and other infrastructure systems was seen as crucial for the nation state to function. Millward on the other hand puts more emphasis on the promotion of social and political unification in general as an explanation of the public-sector interest in these sectors. At the same time, Millward downplays the importance of traditional economic arguments based on natural monopoly argumentation.

Based on the views presented above, an approach has been compiled and is presented in Fig. 3.7, which includes the different factors influencing the development of transport infrastructure systems, a continuous evolution process and the balance over time between private sector provision and public-sector involvement.

If the government decides to organize the system as part of the government sector it has, in line with Chandler's argumentation, a role to set the organization in a way that gives the best possible prerequisites for coordination and efficiency. If private sector provision is favored a proper institutional setting for promoting efficiency by market actors must be set up and fostered by the government. The government's choice between market and hierarchy will be made in an environment where technology, the prevailing transaction costs, the development of the market, and political factors play important roles.

It can of course be discussed whether transport infrastructure systems have been developed in a linear successive process, as suggested in Fig. 3.7. A stepwise approach, with equilibriums that are punctuated and subsequent moves to new phases, seems to be a more accurate

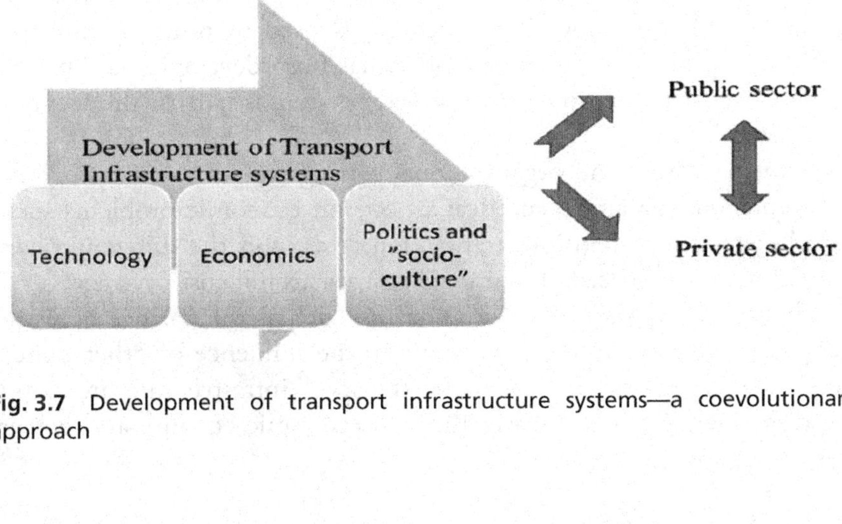

Fig. 3.7 Development of transport infrastructure systems—a coevolutionary approach

description of the development. The introduction of new technology such as railroad and cars represent two such development steps. The straight arrow in the figure might represent a continuous drive for evolution of the transport infrastructure system over time and is therefore used for illustrative purposes here.

Technology, economics (here in a broad sense including a number of financial and organizational aspects), and politics are three important factors influencing the development, but not necessarily as distinct as they are depicted in the illustration. It is probably more accurate to see these factors as blurred and interdependent rather than separate and distinct. A classic take on similar issues is of course the Marxian view that the technologies shape the economic and organizational settings, which in turn has a relationship with and frames the functioning of the political system. Harvey (1989) discusses urban growth in the Western world economies based on Marxist theory and discusses infrastructure development as one of the capital accumulation processes in such a view.

The different factors in the coevolutionary model cover the following aspects:

Technology covers the physical networks of roads and railroads but also the rolling stock (trains) and vehicles, the technological evolution of which has often changed competitive relations between transport modes. Another important example in this category is traffic management systems: either manual or IT-based. Lately, Intelligent Transport Systems (ITS) technology, by which IT is used in order to improve traffic management in congested cities, has been developing as an area drawing a lot of attention, which could be seen as part of the technology factor.

Economics covers the organizational settings as such, but also economic phenomena and theoretical aspects on economic problems such as scale effects, competition, transaction costs, and the different views on pricing policies based on marginal cost versus full cost coverage.

Politics and socio-culture cover questions such as the balance between markets versus government intervention, the influence of other policy areas such as regional policy in the transport infrastructure area, and questions such as the view over time on economic equality and power distribution between local, regional, national, and international organizational levels.

Over time, there has been interplay between the private sector actors, for example, construction companies and technology providers such as Ericsson and Asea (Swedish forerunner of ABB), and the government agencies. This is represented by the interconnecting arrow between private and public-sector alternatives in Fig. 3.7. Kaijser (1994) discusses this interplay as a sign of a "Swedish model" for the provision of infrastructure systems in Sweden. This includes that the government sets up an agency that is responsible for the national infrastructure assets, while responsibility for regional and local networks are given to local governments and private sector actors. An informal cooperation between the actors and the lack of government supervisory agencies overseeing the different subsectors are additional aspects of this view on infrastructure systems, different from Ruiter's (above) suggestion with a hybrid form in-between public and private, which might be similar to Wagner's intertwined view. Ottosson (1997) discusses Sweden's choice of a railroad organization as a midpoint between the centrist Prussian model and the more market leaning British organization model. Furthermore, this seems to be an example of a Swedish model between more single-sided market or government cases.

There is also an interest in the development of different governance forms between public and private sectors in literature discussing multilevel governance (Peters and Pierre 2004). Osborne (2009) discusses the introduction of new management and collaboratory regimes in the relationship between the public and private sectors. The use of PPPs is among the issues raised by Osborne in this respect.

A concluding remark is that economics and economic theory display a number of different views which correspond to the time, scope, and scale aspects of transport infrastructure. It seems to be an inherent difficulty to combine different views on systems like these where stationary balance is followed by change and forming of new structures. In the following chapter, a connected discussion on planning and coordination will add to the complexities related to transport infrastructure theorizing over time.

References

Andersson-Skog, L. (1993). *Såsom allmänna inrättningar till gagnet, men affärsföretag till namnet: SJ, järnvägspolitiken och den ekonomiska omvandlingen efter 1920*. Aa Umeå.

Bergh van den, J., & Stagl, S. (2003). Coevolution of Economic Behavior and Institutions: Towards a Theory of Institutional Change. *Journal of Evolutionary Economics, 13*(3), 289–317.

Blankart, C. B., & Fasten, E. R. (2011). Knut Wicksell's Principle of Just Taxation Revisited. In V. Caspari (Ed.), *The Evolution of Economic Theory Essays in Honour of Bertram Schefold* (pp. 132–141). London: Routledge.

Blaug, M. (2007). The Fundamental Theories of Modern Welfare Economics, Historically Contemplated. *History of Political Economy, 39*(2), 185–207.

Bogart, D. (2009). Nationalizations and the Development of Transport Systems: Cross-Country Evidence from Railroad Networks, 1860–1912. *The Journal of Economic History, 69*(1), 202–237.

Buchanan, J. M. (1968/1999). *The Demand and Supply of Public Goods*. USA: Liberty Fund.

Buchanan, J. M. & Tullock, G. (1962). *The Calculus of Consent: Logical Foundations of Constitutional Democracy* (Vol. 100). Ann Arbor: University of Michigan Press.

Chandler, A. D. (1977). *The Visible Hand: The Managerial Revolution in American Business*. Cambridge, MA, USA: The Belknap Press of Harvard University Press.

Chandler, A. D. (1990). *Scale and Scope: The Dynamics of Industrial Capitalism*. Cambridge, MA, USA: The Belknap Press of Harvard University Press.

Chandler, A. D. (1992). Capabilities and the Economic History of Industrial Enterprise. *The Journal of Economic Perspectives, 6*(3), 79–100.

Clifton, J., Lanthier, P., & Schröter, H. (2011). Regulating and Deregulating the Public Utilities 1830–2010. *Business History, 53*(5), 659–672.

Coase, R. H. (1937). The Nature of the Firm. *Economica, New Series, 4*(16), 386–405.

Coase, R. H. (1946). The Marginal Cost Controversy. *Economica, New Series, 13*(51), 169–182.

Coase, R. H. (1947). The Marginal Cost Controversy: Some Further Comments. *Economica, New Series, 14*(54), 150–153.

Gruber, J. (2011). *Public Finance and Public Policy*. New York, USA: Worth Publishers.

Harvey, D. (1989). *The Urban Experience*. UK: The John Hopkins University Press.

Hasselgren, B. (2011). En mer effektiv transportinfrastruktur. *Ekonomisk Debatt, 39*(6), 20–34.

Hayek, F. A. (1944). *The Road to Serfdom, Text and Documents* (B. Caldwell, Ed. (2007)). Chicago: University of Chicago Press.

Hayek, F. A. (1984). *Der Strom der Güter und Leistungen* (Vol. 101). Tübingen, Germany: Mohr Siebeck.

Hernes, T. (2008). *Understanding Organization as Process—Theory for a Tangled World*. Oxon, UK: Routledge.

Hotelling, H. (1938). The General Welfare in Relation to Problems of Taxation and of Railway and Utility Rates. *Econometrica: Journal of the Econometric Society, 6*(3), 242–269.

Huerta de Soto, J. (2010). *The Austrian School*. Cheltenham, UK and Northampton, USA: Edward Elgar.

Kaijser, A. (1994). *I fädrens spår…*. Stockholm: Carlssons Bokförlag.

Kaijser, A. (2004). The Dynamics of Infrasystems: Lessons from History. *Proceedings of the 6th International Summer Academy on Technology Studies—Urban Infrastructure in Transition*.

Klein, P. G. (1998). New Institutional Economics. *Encyclopedia of Law and Economics 1*, 456–489.

Klein, D. B. (2012). *Knowledge and Coordination—A Liberal Interpretation*. New York: Oxford University Press Inc.

Laffont, J. J., & Tirole, J. (1993). *A Theory of Incentives in Procurement and Regulation*. Cambridge, USA: MIT Press.

Langlois, R. N. (1992). Transaction-cost Economics in Real Time. *Industrial and Corporate Change, 1*(1) 99–127.

Langlois, R. N. (2003). *Chandler in a Larger Frame: Markets, Transaction Costs and Organizational Form in History* (Economics Working Papers No. 16). University of Connecticut.

Leflavie, X. (1996). Organization as Structures of Domination. *Organization Studies, 17*(1), 23–47.

McCarthy, P. S. (2001). *Transportation Economics: Theory and Practice: A Case Study Approach*. Malden, MA: Wiley-Blackwell.

McCloskey, N. D. (2010). *Bourgeois Dignity: Why Economics Can't Explain the Modern World*. Chicago, USA and London, UK: Chicago University Press.

Medema, S. G. (2009). *The Hesitant Hand, Taming Self-interest in the History of Economic Ideas*. Princeton, USA: Princeton University Press.

Merkert, R. (2009). *The Organization of European Railways: A Transaction Cost Perspective*. The University of Leeds Institute for Transport Studies.

Milgrom, P. R., & Roberts, J. (1992). *Economics, Organization and Management*. Englewood Cliffs, NJ: Prentice Hall.

Millward, R. (2005). *Private and Public Enterprise in Europe*. UK: Cambridge University Press.

Millward, R. (2011). Public Enterprise in the Modern Western World: An Historical Analysis. *Annals of Public and Cooperative Economics, 82*(4), 378–398.

Mokyr, J. (1990). *The Lever of Riches: Technological Creativity and Economic Progress*. Oxford, UK: Oxford University Press.

Mosca, M. (2008). On the Origins of the Concept of Natural Monopoly: Economies of Scale and Competition. *The European Journal of the History of Economic Thought, 15*(2), 317–353.

Nelson, R., & Winter, S. (1982). *An Evolutionary Theory of Economic Change*. Cambridge, MA: Belknap Press of Harvard University Press.

Newbery, D. M. (1990). Pricing and Congestion: Economic Principles Relevant to Pricing Roads. *Oxford Review of Economic Policy, 5*(2), 22–38.

North, D. C. (1990). *Institutions, Institutional Change and Economic Performance*. Cambridge, UK: Cambridge University Press.

Osborne, S. (Ed.). (2009). *The New Public Governance: Emerging Perspectives on the Theory and Practice of Public Governance*. London and New York: Routledge.

Ostrom, E. (2005). *Understanding Institutional Diversity*. Princeton, NJ: Princeton University Press.

Ottosson, J. (1997). Path Dependence and Institutional Evolution: The Case of the Nationalisation of Private Railroads in Interwar Sweden. In L. Magnusson & J. Ottosson (Eds.), *Evolutionary Economics and Path Dependence* (pp. 186–196). Cheltenham: Edward Elgar.

Parry, I. W., & Bento, A. (2001). Revenue Recycling and the Welfare Effects of Road Pricing. *The Scandinavian Journal of Economics, 103*(4), 645–671.

Pennington, M. (2004). Citizen Participation, the 'Knowledge Problem' and Urban Land Use Planning: An Austrian Perspective. *The Review of Austrian Economics, 17*(2), 213–231.

Pennington, M. (2011). *Robust Political Economy, Classical Liberalism and the Future of Public Policy*. Cheltenham, UK: Edward Elgar

Peters, B. G., & Pierre, J. (2004). Multi-level Governance and Democracy: A Faustian Bargain? In I. Bache & M. Flinders (Eds.), *Multi-level Governance*. Oxford: Oxford University Press.

Rietveld, P. (2012). Barrier Effects of Borders: Implications for Borders: Implications for Border-Crossing Infrastructure. *European Journal for Transport Infrastructure and Research, 12*(2), 150–166.

Rietveld, P., & Stough, R. (2007). *Institutions and Sustainable Transport: Regulatory Reform in Advanced Economies*. Cheltenham, UK and Northhampton, USA: Edward Elgar.

Ruggles, N. (1949). The Welfare Basis of the Marginal Cost Principle. *Review of Economic Studies, 17*(1), 29–46.

Ruiter, D. (2005). Is Transaction Cost Economics Applicable to Public Governance? *European Journal of Law and Economics, 20*(3), 287–303.

Sager, T. (2012). *Reviving Critical Planning Theory*. London: Routledge.

Schumpeter, J. A. (1942/2008). *Capitalism, Socialism and Democracy*. New York: Harper Perennial Modern Thought.

Schumpeter, J. A. (1950). The March Into Socialism. *The American Economic Review, 40*(2), 446–456.

Tunzelmann von, N. (2003). Historical Co-evolution of Governance and Technology in the Industrial Revolutions. *Structural Change and Economic Dynamics, 14*(4), 365–384.

Wagner, R. E. (Ed.). (1991/2011). *Charging for Government: User Charges and Earmarked Taxes in Principle and Practice*. New York, USA: Routledge Revivals.

Wagner, R. E. (2007). *Fiscal Sociology and the Theory of Public Finance—An Exploratory Essay*. Northhampton, USA: Edward Elgar.

Williamson, O. E. (1981). The Economics of Organization: The Transaction Cost Approach. *The American Journal of Sociology, 87*(3), 548–577.

Williamson, O. E. (1999). Public and Private Bureaucracies: A Transaction Cost Economics Perspective. *The Journal of Law, Economics and Organization, 15*(1), 306–342.

Williamson, O. E. (2000). The New Institutional Economics: Taking Stock, Looking Ahead. *Journal of Economic Literature, 38*(3), 595–613.

Winston, C. (1991). Efficient Transportation Infrastructure Policy. *The Journal of Economic Perspectives, 5*(1), 113–127.

Zappia, C. (2001). Equilibrium and Disequilibrium Dynamics in the 1930s. *Journal of the History of Economic Thought, 23*(1), 55–75.

4

Planning and Coordination of Transport Infrastructure

This chapter deals with the planning aspects of transport infrastructure systems. It discusses two pairs of dimensions that are important when dealing with these issues. On the one hand is a balance between markets and public-sector organizations. On the other hand is the balance between centralized and decentralized forms of organization of transport infrastructure systems and infrastructure planning. Examples from the current situation in the USA and in the EU are used as examples of organizational models.

Planning has to do with change from a present situation to a desired future state. Planning has connections to actors' perceptions, abilities, and goal structures, but also to the view on information and its deeper use and understanding in the form of knowledge. To a large extent, planning also has to do with coordination of resources and actions. In the current literature, transport infrastructure planning and transport policy issues are closely intertwined. To begin with, mainstream planning literature is in general focused on the understanding of the flaws connected to public-sector planning and the further development of the public-sector planners' traditional role. For example, how should public-sector planners as experts be able to refine their

B. Hasselgren, *Transport Infrastructure in Time, Scope and Scale*,
https://doi.org/10.1007/978-3-319-79054-1_4

practices with the help of improved forecasting techniques, developed cost–benefit analysis, and more refined strategic planning practices and systems? Questions such as these are asked by scholars like Banister (2002), Button and Hensher (2005), Flyvbjerg (2007a, b), and Kölbl et al. (2008).

Short and Kopp (2005) have focused on the different geographical levels in transport infrastructure policies, arguing for further research into planning practices at different levels, specifically focusing on supranational planning methods and practices. Banister and Hickman (2012) have joined those who strive for refinement of planning methods by arguing for further exploitation of scenario technique in strategic planning.

Furthermore, the interest in understanding the politics and economics of mega projects has also grown into a research area of its own. With the view that we will probably see more and more major or "mega-sized" transport infrastructure projects in the future, and based on the experience from having the "wrong" projects prioritized and later constructed, often with major cost-overruns, this has become a pressing area to explore. Here, perhaps contributions by Altschuler and Luberoff (2003), Bruzelius et al. (2002), and Flyvbjerg (1998) reflecting on different mega projects, political processes, and risks stand out as the most prominent contributions.

Flyvbjerg often focuses on the striking irrationality of decision processes around mega projects with a "strategic misrepresentation" of pro-project interest in the public-sector environment and with an outcome leading to the "survival of the unfittest" projects. Flyvbjerg (2007a) has suggested strengthening incentives for efficiency through improved accountability and developed critical public review processes as remedies. Altschuler and Luberoff have included more public choice-related explanations for the functioning of the processes around mega projects with private sector rent seekers and public-sector entrepreneurs, both easily recognizable actors in these projects. Van Wee (2007) among many others has added to the analysis by suggesting measures for strengthening the planning and forecasting methodologies in the tradition of the mainstream literature in the group of theories above.

Even if most of the scholars in the current literature have an interest in the development of planning, and indeed discuss and try to find remedies to flaws, there are only few examples where a discussion on knowledge as a prerequisite for successful coordination is clearly discussed. Here, it is argued that the possibility to access and gather knowledge is crucial for a deepened understanding of transport infrastructure planning.

4.1 Knowledge and Coordination

Transport infrastructure systems have to be planned, whether they are provided and managed by the public sector or by the private sector. The new transportation systems, here primarily roads and railroads, introduced in the nineteenth and twentieth centuries brought to the fore new coordination and planning issues. Planning in the transport infrastructure sector is often concerned with the long-term physical and economic planning of extensions of the road and railroad networks. Yet, it can also include activities directed at arriving at a situation with more efficient management of the current networks.

Technology (signaling, bridge capacity, etc.) and quality aspects must be coordinated and new construction, reinvestments, and maintenance must be organized and carried out in a timely manner. Regulation to safeguard traffic safety or the efficient use of the roads and railroads must also be coordinated. Scale effects are, by definition, captured only as resources are combined or the same resources used for different purposes, generally as an effect of coordination.

Information about a large number of different aspects related to the road and railroad systems is necessary to be able to plan activities in the future and the present. This information must be transformed into a deeper understanding of circumstances that are important for the activity that an actor is intending to carry out. This deeper understanding based on information is captured by the knowledge concept. This might be seen as the sum pieces of data, information and experience put together to create patterns of thinking and theorizing around society and economic activity.

Langlois and Nelson and Winter have been pointed to earlier as examples of scholars signaling an interest for the generation of knowledge and capabilities through learning in organizations. Hayek (1945) discussed the possible use of and capability among centralized planners to obtain the necessary knowledge in order to be able to take correct decisions in a classical article in the field, The Use of Knowledge in Society. Hayek argued for a cautious view on these possibilities, furthering a view where knowledge is dispersed at the local and individual levels in society rather than at aggregate levels. According to this view, aggregated knowledge is available more as an end result of market exchange than as a result of centralized planning.

When the infrastructure system covers more than one jurisdictional area, the coordination of the systems includes more difficult aspects such as different institutional settings, language, culture, and different priorities set in relation to the same project. There is also a tendency for every separate jurisdiction to try to reap the advantages of transport infrastructure measures while finding ways to having other jurisdictions to pay for the same measures. These aspects are also discussed in the theoretical field of fiscal federalism, that is discussing prospects for finding efficient functioning of public-sector organizations affected by both politics and self-interest in the public administration, two of the obstacles against an efficient public-sector organization (Oates 2005). Hayek (1960) and Tiebout (1956) have also discussed the prospects of organizing public-sector organizations at the local level, with Hayek seeing local government as a better alternative than central government and Tiebout pointing to the competition between different local jurisdictions as important for efficiency in the public sector.

Viewed from one side of a national border, a project might show very different potentialities than another. As an example, the interest from the southern Swedish region Skåne to connect to the Danish capital Copenhagen with its supply of a wide range of services and goods might be very different from the Danish interest in connecting to Skåne and Sweden's third-largest city Malmö, a medium-sized regional city with only few additional qualities to offer, save for perhaps low-wage workers and nice holiday surroundings.

A number of these barriers to cross-border infrastructure have been discussed recently by Rietveld (2012), who points to a number of institutional difficulties such as regulation, but also to different preferences and the lack of information about the situation in the other country. The knowledge aspect is clearly an important part of the understanding of these strategic infrastructure systems and how coordination can be realized. Klein (2012) points to the situation wherein coordination can be interpreted as having two different meanings. On the one hand, Klein argues that the combination of different activities and factors (*concatenate coordination*), originally within a firm and later on a wider scale in the economy, in order to arrive at some higher level of "effective arrangement" (p. 37) is an example of a combinatory focus that the term "coordination" originally had in economics. This transitive meaning of the verb to coordinate also makes intentionality a central aspect. Someone must coordinate in the firm or in society at large. How this coordination activity comes about, either centrally or spontaneously, can be seen as the basic aspect in many discussions around planning, for example, in the debate on market socialism during the 1930–1940.

Since the 1960s, Klein argues that the meaning of coordination has changed to focus more on *mutual coordination*, an intransitive verb, where the interrelation with other actors or systems is instead the central aspect of coordination. This is also what is generally analyzed in game theory, even if Klein argues that mutual coordination has also become the main understanding of coordination in other areas such as macroeconomics. Perhaps coordination in the latter form could also be seen to fit closer with different communicative views on coordination and planning, whereby efficient solutions of planning issues (often in a local setting) are sought without always taking the overriding efficient use of resources into consideration. Here, the main question and purpose are to analyze how in a system like transport infrastructure, an economizing (or efficient) use of the available resources comes about. Another interest is to analyze how the process of arriving at such a state can be understood or arranged. Processes and institutions fostering learning and economizing behavior are thus in focus. It seems like coordination of the concatenate type would be the one most close to this purpose.

Klein (2012) suggests that optimization or efficiency should perhaps be altered for "pleasing arrangements" (p. 37) when moving from the firm level to an economic system level. This is a view that reflects one of the characteristics of the institutional paradigm. A similar view also seems reasonable with regard to transport infrastructure planning. In a small project like minor road construction, it might be possible to optimize resource utilization, such as cost reduction given a defined project aim. However, moving upwards in the system, optimization or even a reasonably vaguely defined efficiency, is more and more difficult to observe and evaluate, as complexities increase both internally in the system and externally.

External influences, initiated by, for example, the political system or coming from counterparts in the projects, make the planning environment more and more complex. The cost of coordination is raised in a study comparing the functioning of the public transit systems of the San Francisco Bay Area and of the Washington, DC area (Chisholm 1989). One conclusion is that the relatively fragmented system in the Bay Area in the 1980s seems to have achieved a satisfactory level of efficiency and coordination at a reasonable cost. The tendency for amalgamation of previously more decentralized and multifaceted structures in public transport in the USA, into larger "Metropolitan Transportation Commissions," is studied. These have often been labeled as improving coordination by stronger hierarchy.

Yet, Chisholm concludes that the probable costs of improving coordination through government intervention and the introduction of hierarchy as the organizational principle instead of spontaneity are probably a case of exponential cost growth rather than linear. Therefore, there are some signs that planned hierarchical coordination has an increasing cost bias rather than the opposite. An important aspect of planning for transport infrastructure is negotiation between actors who operate at different organizational levels in the transport system. Negotiations can also be seen as an expression of coordination, whereby the most efficient use of existing or new assets is sought. Negotiations can, according to Raiffa et al. (2002), from an analytical standpoint be divided into either a distributional or an integrative realm. Distributional negotiations are about sharing the values that are at stake among the negotiating parties, with a focus mainly on the split between the parties of whatever there is to divide. This can be a monetary value, power, influence, or perhaps moral justice.

Integrative negotiations are defined by Raiffa et al. as those situations or processes where the parties engage primarily in shaping values that are larger than in the original situation. Raiffa et al. (2002) argue that integrative negotiations are centered on capabilities and resources among the parties. It is about "integrating the parties' capabilities and resources to generate more value" (p. 97).

Raiffa et al. also exemplify the two basic models by explaining that distributive negotiations are about the division of goods more than value creation. Distributive negotiations, which can be expected to dominate in a system with central government financing provided to lower levels in the system, might be seen as a parallel to Klein's suggested mutual coordination stance. Integrative negotiations might be closer to a concatenate coordination stance. The zero-sum game's stylish distributive form of negotiations could be expected to be connected to government dominated planning modes, with their connections to politics. Market-based solutions are, on the other hand, more focused on value creation, which is the basis for exchange. Whether strong institutional arrangements are in place to foster exchange and learning could, from this point of view, be what decides whether market failure or spontaneous ordering is the outcome of these negotiations. Over time, it can be argued that different distributional aspects of mutual coordination have been brought more to the fore, also in transport infrastructure planning. This has also become the core focus of many policy decisions and processes related to transport infrastructure in many countries.

Figure 4.1 shows four modes of planning in terms of the two pairs: coordination and knowledge. The upper two modes represent ideal planning modes, where some sort of optimization, given the resources and knowledge available, is achieved.

The lower two modes represent either market failure, here in terms of an uncoordinated less efficient result, and government failure, also in terms of lacking coordination. Failures can of course be the result of a number of different reasons. With regard to market failure, the absence of an institutional setting with defined property rights, weak contract

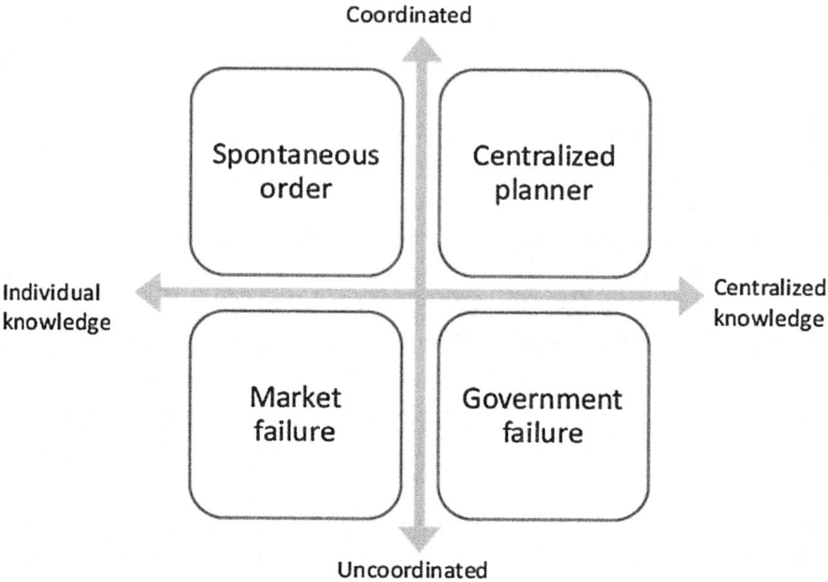

Fig. 4.1 Four modes of transport infrastructure planning

law or low confidence between actors in the markets might make the economy operate at a less than optimal (or pleasing) level. Furthermore, government failure might be connected to unsuccessful planning or an individual (public official's or politician's private) preference orientation rather than a general or objective preference orientation.

While the two upper modes can be seen as idealized examples of textbook versions of well-coordinated situations, the two failure modes are more likely to occur in either the less than rational world governments face and/or taking into account the many possible obstacles toward a spontaneous order (or Hayekian catallaxy) setting. Such obstacles might originate from government regulation that distorts price signals in the economy. The many difficulties connected to arriving at a situation where a centralized planner provides a well-coordinated outcome have been described in a number of cases. A centralized government planner would have difficulties obtaining information about the transport infrastructure system as such. Many times, the very diversified and elaborated political aim structures as such as exemplified in Chapter 1 are another challenge when trying to convert these into real policies. These often lead to a number of goal conflicts that are difficult to balance.

Trade-offs between regional policy aims, which work in favor of decentralized systems, and transport flow economizing leading to centralization are only one such nearly unsolvable conflict. The measurement of road and railroad users' marginal utility valuations is another difficult area for a centralized planner. The many obstacles to the success of a centralized planner have been discussed by Coase (1946) and Hayek (1944, 1945). Since then the discussion on limitations on planning and rationality as the main organizational idea has been a common theme in a vast amount literature. March and Simon (1958) made an important contribution to this literature and provided a starting point for a view on organizations as a fluid process rather than a strict bureaucracy, a theme that has been followed and developed by many scholars.

The centralized planner mode can also be seen as connected to neoclassical welfare economics theory with its focus on equilibrium analysis based on the assumption of unitary and rather stable utility functions among users over time. With the positivist assumption being the basis of these theories, it is also an integral view that once the proper analytical tools are taken into use there is always a possibility that an optimization might finally be reached by a centralized planner. The widespread uses of social cost–benefit analysis and the ongoing methodological development of this model as currently carried out in research and practiced by institutions as the Swedish Transport Administration (Trafikverket 2012), are examples of activities and methods connected to the neoclassical paradigm but are also closely connected to the centralized planner mode. The examples given from current planning literature above also point to the strength of this orientation.

The standard solution of handling a situation where a natural monopoly exists, a basic tenet of neoclassic theory, is to regulate or nationalize the assets and operations of the area. This would, in principle, allow for the efficient use of resources, based on marginal cost pricing and deficit funding by the government, as discussed earlier. Why a government monopoly would be more efficient than a possible private sector monopoly, or whether regulation should be focused on preserving or shaping at least oligopolistic competition, is seldom answered.

This solution, although it is often seen as a measure to reach some kind of optimization, is generally, one where the deficiencies of the centralized planner mode are obvious. Natural monopolies do not generally exist other than for some specific section or aspect of a transport infrastructure system, and they change over time. Nationalization as a solution to a perceived natural monopoly situation is, however, a measure that has generally a long-lasting effect, shaping paths for future action. What might be seen as short-term improvement is therefore often transformed into a long-term failure.

The possibility fostering a move from a situation characterized by market or government failure to one where market forces work more freely is often suggested when reforming economies and societies characterized by rigid structures and low growth rates. Those policies generally aim to make use of markets' ability to allow for innovativeness and dynamism, which is in turn connected to the decentralized knowledge that is a sign of this model. These solutions usually aim for entrepreneurship and experimentation, but they are also part of the theories that discuss the functioning of spontaneous orders. A better use of the available resources through a market system based on prices signaling supply and demand of goods and services, rather than plans based on projections by centralized planners, is often the purpose of these policies.

A crucial prerequisite for spontaneous ordering is the existence of an institutional framework, where the government has a role to safeguard the functioning of the system. Comparative studies with a focus on institutional settings have been carried out by a number of scholars, among which North (1990) has presented important insights. Besides the formal institutional framework, informal and cultural aspects also contribute to forming a stable environment for markets to function. A take on these different systems and their interrelations has been provided by Williamson (2000), as mentioned above, in which norms and traditions such as formal rules like proprietary rights operate at an over-layered level in any society, structures which change only slowly. These layers of institutions are connected to more short-lived structures such as governance structures, transaction costs, and at the basic level production functions and resource allocation arrangements at lower levels of the model.

Over time, we can see that transportation systems have become more and more elaborated with growing scale and scope complexities. This institutionalization of the sector has grown hand in hand with an increased need for planning as complex dilemmas around how to acheive a good resource allocation have become more common. The nation has over time been a natural level of these developments. More and more often it is though the case that transport infrastructure planning has to come about also on a level above the nation or state. This tendency is discussed in the next section.

4.2 The Spatial Dimension

The successive opening of the national transport markets in the EU for cross-border transport and the growing transport flows connected to increasing specialization in the European economy (as an effect of the internal market) is changing the preconditions for the organization of an efficient transport infrastructure system. In an earlier stage of European integration, efficiencies of scale were captured mainly at the national level in the transport system. In this development, the interplay between the national and the supranational level is increasingly important in the development of transport infrastructure systems. International cooperation and coordination can be expected to bring a need for more stringent and clear-cut national policies and strategies with regard to transport infrastructure. More cross-border related transport projects than earlier are discussed as the international exchange increases. Physical transportation connections to other EU member states are growing in importance.

Examples of projects where an international focus and participation are necessary are Öresundsbron, Svinesundsbron (both major bridges between Sweden and Denmark/Norway), and the Baltic Sea Strategy, as well as Trans-European Networks for Transport (TEN-T) policies at large. Currently, for Scandinavia, many of these issues relate to connections to Denmark and through the coming Fehmarn Belt tunnel from

Denmark to Germany, also with the European transport systems. The improvement of the railroad connection from Malmö in Sweden to Oslo in Norway is also a related project. Matthiessen, Andersson and Andersson (2013) and Remmo (2012) have discussed several aspects in relation to these extensions, pointing to their value for long-term growth policies and calling for government action. A similar process has taken place for other EU member states and, at a federal/state level, in the USA with a gradual development of transport infrastructure systems organized at different levels in the system, and with a major role for the EU/federal level. In both the EU and the USA, efficiencies of scale are present at the level above rather than at the national/state level.

It could be argued that similar discussions and aims to those currently on the agenda in the EU affected the discussion and decisions to develop a system of national roads in the USA in the 1950s. Among the purposes of the Interstate Highway System decisions was the idea of strengthening the US internal market based on increased trade flows and personal mobility. Recently, the increasing difficulties in preserving a sustainable federal funding system in the USA has led to growing dependency on state and local funding and a reintroduction of private sector funding of the highway system (as PPPs and tolls). Compared to the EU's situation, this discussion about the future concerns of the already established interstate system is seen by most observers as sufficient in its basic structure, though lacking in capacity and resources for maintenance in many urban areas, with resulting heavy congestion in a number of places and a deteriorating quality.

There seems to be need for discussing the level above the nation states in the EU or the states in federal systems. The next section deals with these questions and the prospects for transport infrastructure planning at different spatial levels.

4.3 Recent Trends in the EU and the USA

The current development in the EU and the USA with regard to transport infrastructure shows some signs of contradiction. The USA seems to be heading for decentralization in the road system, while the EU seems to be strengthening the centralized coordination. The core question here, with the focus on strategic planning, is how the necessary coordination in order to achieve an efficient use of resources should be arranged? Could an efficient or at least satisfactory coordination come about through centralized government intervention or rather through decentralization to lower levels in the system?

Since the 1950s, the USA has had a stronger central government-led coordination of road planning and regulation than in earlier periods. Its interstate system and the methods for road planning were (Hasselgren 2013), seen as the most modern among the countries in the Western world, as Sweden and other countries in Europe developed its strategic road planning methods in the 1950s. In a time of financial austerity, the US federal Highway Trust Fund is, however, under pressure. A solution that could gradually evolve from this situation seems to be that states and regions would take on stronger responsibility for the interstate highways, in many cases opening for alternative financing through tolls and PPPs.

At the same time, the transport infrastructure planning and financing in the EU seems to be going in another direction. While still being dominated by member states financing, the European Commission and its Innovations & Networks Executive Agency (INEA) are fostering stronger coordinative measures in order to facilitate the construction of missing links in the core network of TEN-T roads and railroads, since a number of years within a transport corridor framework. A number of technology-enhancing and regulative measures allowing for the internal market to function better through stronger competition, for example, are also part of the EU's policies in the sector. Private sector financing and private actors will also probably play more important roles in the future as part of these measures.

The USA and EU seem thus to be taking different steps to achieve the necessary coordination in a situation with financial distress. The change in the USA from stronger federal government coordination of interstate highways toward more of state and regional initiatives, and a growing proportion of financing coming from user fees, also seems to be in line with more local initiatives and based on more local knowledge. Lower spatial levels in the system could in parallel to the earlier discussion generally be expected to have access to wider knowledge bases than higher levels. At the same time, the coordination potential might be limited on local as compared to central levels in the systems.

The development in the USA seems primarily to represent a horizontal move from one level of government administration to another spatial level of government administration, as displayed in Fig. 4.2. It could be argued that this will likely lead to new examples of government failure, as viewed from the perspective of knowledge and coordination, but at a lower spatial level in the system. Even if some of the decisions will be better informed than earlier, the potential gains from a strategic planning and management at a level above the states might be reduced. The system might end up with higher quality decisions at a suboptimal level in terms of the strategic issues. These are some of the issues discussed by Tiebout and Hayek (see above) in their discussion on local versus central responsibility for sectors in the economy with public goods characteristics.

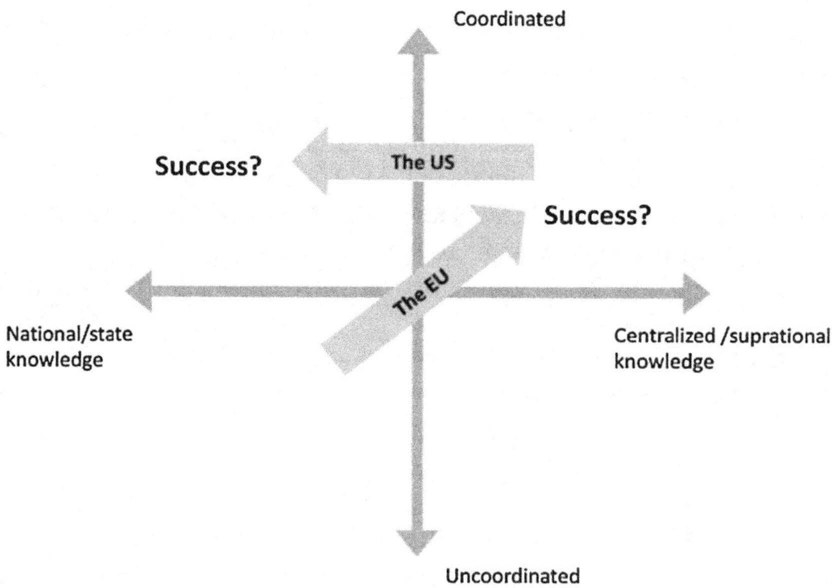

Fig. 4.2 Centralization and decentralization of transport infrastructure issues

In terms of the knowledge/coordination aspects, the tendency for centralization in the EU might be described as a vertical move upwards in the public administration system as displayed in Fig. 4.2. The prospects for achieving a coordinated situation will probably improve, from an EU perspective, compared to the former situation with less focused EU policies and measures in the area. At the same time, the centralized planning mode sought after through this change might represent a situation where new government failure at a more centralized spatial level in the system might be the effect. The lack of appropriate data and planning processes both at national and supranational levels in OECD countries, and exemplified by many of the major EU countries, has been observed by Short and Kopp (2005) reporting to the European Conference of Ministers of Transport (ECMT).

Short and Kopp found a number of different planning methods in different countries, a lack of data to base decisions on, a highly politicized decision process, and a weak interest to follow up and evaluate implemented decisions. At the supranational planning level, Short and Kopp report (p. 364) "analytic weaknesses" also present at the national level, "processes becoming political and politicized to the point where national pride was at stake," and that "It was inevitable that project benefits were over-emphasized." There still seems to be a lack of common understanding on which planning efforts should be carried out at a supranational level. The findings seem to underpin the difficulties connected to centralized government planning at both a national and supranational spatial level.

A contradicting view would of course be that centralized strategic planning efforts in the USA have without question been an important part of the success of having the Interstate Highway System constructed. Without this centralization, the system would probably have been developed slower and perhaps without the national perspective. And it could of course be argued that had the EU worked more strategically with TEN-T development and planning, at least since the 1980s when the EU's internal market focus was strengthened, EU-wide transportation systems would probably have been much more well-developed than today.

Part of the centralized strategic planning paradigm in the USA has at the same time been a degree of inflexibility toward local town planning. The political processes with many kinds of negotiations carried out when it comes to financing, coalition building, and local town planning issues related to the Big Dig project in Boston, MA, has been described by Altshuler and Luberoff (2003). Similar insights have been reported by Glaeser (2011), who discusses how cities can succeed but often fail when it comes to urban planning initiatives, including transport infrastructure. Apart from exemplifying the difficulties with implementing a one-size-fits-all policy throughout the USA, numerous examples of mutual (distributive) rather than concatenate (integrative) planning, and negotiation games are exemplified by these scholars.

A line of reasoning supporting more strategic and active coordination in the EU is that other projects would have been prioritized in the EU with such a strategic coordination, possibly with drastically lower investments in the Mediterranean countries and possibly more investments in the more heavily populated areas. From a macroeconomic and growth-oriented point of view, this might have given a better result than the present situation, where heavy (over) spending in countries like Greece, Spain, and Portugal in transport infrastructure might explain part of these countries' recent fiscal difficulties.

This might, however, not give the complete picture. A crucial question, from knowledge/coordination-perspective, is instead whether a strategy for transport infrastructure development that would have leaned more toward the spontaneous ordering model might have led to different priorities than those chosen both in the EU and in the USA. It could be argued that the EU development might have been even more focused on road transportation than today, given the high costs of railroad infrastructure with such a planning orientation. Urban sprawl in the USA, as discussed by Glaeser, is perhaps an example of the outcomes of market-led planning. Glaeser though generally gives a broader set of answers to why urban sprawl occurs, market-led urban planning being only one of them.

Winston (2010) describes some of the inefficiencies connected to US highway planning. He exemplifies the inefficiencies with the heavily developed planning bureaucracy, working in a number of organizational layers from the federal down to the local level and the complexities of the funding structure, which make outcomes of federal and state financing difficult to predict. The high degree of discretionary decisions in Congress over transport-related appropriations is another problem that probably lowers the efficiency of the system. Finally, cost-overruns in many investment projects have been a sign of the US system.

The case for leaning more toward a spontaneous market-based view on planning of complex large-scale systems, in some cases connected to urban planning, has been discussed by a number of scholars. Hayek has noted (1944) that transport infrastructure might be an area for government action, and later (1960) argued that there are a number of flaws connected to public-sector town planning such as lack of understanding of proprietary rights, the risk of overregulation and bureaucratization, which makes it less probable to be effective. In the 1960 text, Hayek reflects on the existence of "benefits or harms to others that a property owner may cause" (p. 474), echoing the insights of Coase's (1960) article on the Problem of Social Cost that dealt with such externalities in market settings. Both Hayek and Coase call for the use of stronger proprietary rights and pricing or negotiations for solving these issues. Gruber (2011) and McCarthy (2001) both raise the more or less classical counterarguments to Coasean bargaining such as the difficulty to price externalities and the existence of free riders. The search for solutions to controversies over land use, partly the effect of external costs, is of course one of the core issues in any centralized non-market planning effort, both generally and specifically for transport infrastructure with these systems' many external potential conflicts (Fig. 4.3).

Other scholars have focused more on possible ways of strengthening the spontaneous ordering processes, starting from a Hayek/Coase-style analysis. There seems to be a similarity among those scholars in the view that an alternative to government centralized planning should start from smaller geographical units than generally thought of in transport infrastructure planning. A focus on the local neighborhood, municipality, or community is a common theme for scholars like Klein (2012), Pennington (2002), and Webster (2002). Based on proprietary rights, negotiations and contractual regulation planning issues at higher spatial levels in society are suggested to take place through spontaneous

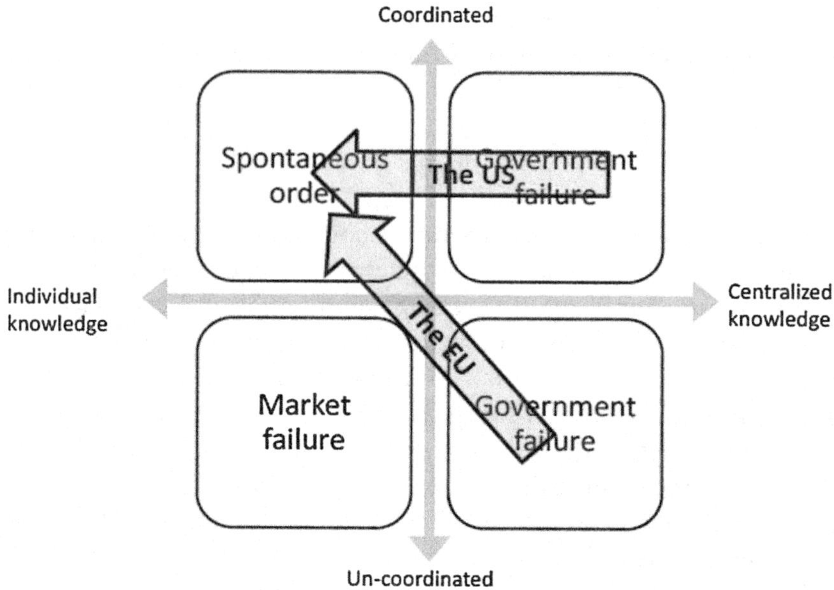

Fig. 4.3 Coordination through spontaneous ordering—a possible way ahead?

"inter-authority bargaining" (Pennington, p. 74) rather than through government planning. A bottom-up perspective seems to be an important feature of such spontaneous order style alternative planning. Webster also points to the probability that club-like structures will likely be part of more such decentralized models for spatial planning issues.

How to arrive at a situation that opens for experimentation and competition between different owners and managers of infrastructure assets is another theme that a number of scholars have raised. Winston (2010) suggests allowing for entrepreneurship and experimentation as the way forward for US transport policy to be revitalized. Market solutions should also be actively sought for to revitalize the transportation sector. The role of the government in a system based on this a decentralized spontaneous ordering planning mode seems to be one of the institution "protector," assuring the proper regulation (including competition regulation) and functioning of the legislative framework, rather than going into details of planning issues.

An important aspect of the spontaneous ordering mode is the probable existence of larger structures organized in order to reduce transaction costs on markets. Firms and other organizations, possibly encompassing wider spatial areas, are but one such possible structure, mentioned by Coase (1937). Therefore, spontaneous ordering is not necessarily seen as identical to small-scale solutions.

References

Altschuler, A., & Luberoff, D. (2003). *Mega Projects—The Changing Politics of Urban Public Investments*. Washington, DC: The Brookings Institution.

Banister, D. (2002). *Transport Planning*. London, UK: Routledge.

Banister, D., & Hickman, R. (2012). Transport Futures: Thinking the Unthinkable. *Transport Policy*. https://doi.org/10.1016/j.tranpol.2012.07.005.

Bruzelius, N., Flyvbjerg, B., & Rothengatter, W. (2002). Big Decisions, Big Risks: Improving Accountability in Mega Projects. *Transport Policy, 9*(2), 143–154.

Button, K. J., & Hensher, D. A. (2005). *Handbook of Transport Strategy: Policy and Institutions*. Oxford: Elsevier.

Chisholm, D. (1989). *Coordination Without Hierarchy, Informal Structures in Multiorganizational Systems*. Berkeley: University of California Press.

Coase, R. H. (1937). The Nature of the Firm. *Economica, New Series, 4*(16), 386–405.

Coase, R. H. (1946). The Marginal Cost Controversy. *Economica, New Series, 13*(51), 169–182.

Coase, R. H. (1960). The Problem of Social Cost. *Journal of Law and Economics, 3*, 1–44.

Flyvbjerg, B. (1998). *Rationality and Power: Democracy in Practice*. Chicago: University of Chicago Press.

Flyvbjerg, B. (2007a). Policy and Planning for Large-Infrastructure Projects: Problems, Causes, Cures. *Environment and Planning B: Planing and Design, 34*(4), 578 ff.

Flyvbjerg, B. (2007b). Truth and Lies About Megaprojects Inaugural Speech, Delft University of Technology.

Glaeser, E. (2011). *Triumph of the City—How Our Greatest Invention Make Us Richer Smarter, Greener, Healthier and Happier*. USA: Penguin Group.

Gruber, J. (2011). *Public Finance and Public Policy*. New York: Worth Publishers.

Hayek, F. A. (1944). *The Road to Serfdom, Text and Documents* (B. Caldwell, Ed. (2007)). Chicago: University of Chicago Press.

Hayek, F. A. (1945). The Use of Knowledge in Society. *American Economic Review, 35*(4), 519–530.

Hayek, F. A. (1960). *The Constitution of Liberty—The Definitive Edition* (R. Hamowy, Ed. (2011)). Chicago: University of Chicago Press.

Hasselgren, B. (2013) *The Reluctant Infrastructure Manager, 70 Years of Government Ownership of Transport Infrastructure in Sweden* (Research Paper). Stockholm: KTH Royal Institute of Technology.

Klein, D. B. (2012). *Knowledge and Coordination—A Liberal Interpretation*. New York: Oxford University Press Inc.

Kölbl, R., Niegl, M., & Knoflacher, H. (2008). A Strategic Planning Methodology. *Transport Policy, 15*(5), 273–282.

March, J. G., & Simon, H. A. (1958). *Organizations*. New York: Wiley.

Matthiessen, C. W., Andersson, Å. E., & Andersson, D. E. (2013). *Öresundsregionen: Den dynamiska Metropolen*. Stockholm: Dialogos Förlag.

McCarthy, P. S. (2001). *Transportation Economics; Theory and Practice: A Case Study Approach*. Malden: Blackwell.

North, D. C. (1990). *Institutions, Institutional Change and Economic Performance*. Cambridge, UK: Cambridge University Press.

Oates, W. E. (2005). Toward a Second-Generation Theory of Fiscal Federalism. *International Tax and Public Finance, 12*(4), 349–373.

Pennington, M. (2002). *Liberating the Land: The Case for Private Land-Use Planning*. London: Institute for Economic Affairs.

Raiffa, H., Richardson, J., & Metcalfe, D. (2002). *Negotiation Analysis*. Cambridge, MA: Harvard University Press.

Remmo, J. (2012). Utmaningar och hinder i gränsöverskridande transport-infrastrukturplanering: En studie av TEN-T med Nordiska triangeln som exempel (Master Thesis, KTH Royal Institute of Technology).

Rietveld, P. (2012). Barrier Effects of Borders: Implications for Borders; Implications for Border-Crossing Infrastructure. *European Journal for Transport Infrastructure and Research, 12*(2), 150–166.

Short, J. and Kopp, A. (2005). Transport Infrastructure: Investment and Planning: Policy and Research Aspects. *Transport Policy 12*(4), 360–367.

Tiebout, C. (1956). A Pure Theory of Local Expenditures. *Journal of Political Economy, 64*(5), 416–424.

Trafikverket (2012). Samhällsekonomiska principer och kalkylvärden för transportsektorn: ASEK 5.

Van Wee, B. (2007). Large Infrastructure Projects: A Review of the Quality of Demand Forecasts and Cost Estimations. *Environment and Planning B: Planning and Design, 34*(4), 611–625.

Webster, C. (2002). Property Rights and the Public Realm: Gates, Green Belts and Gemeinschaft. *Environment and Planning B: Planning and Design, 29*(3), 397–412.

Williamson, O. E. (2000). The New Institutional Economics: Taking Stock, Looking Ahead. *Journal of Economic Literature, 38*(3), 595–613.

Winston, C. (2010). *Last Exit—Privatization and Deregulation of the U.S. Transportation System*. Washington, DC: Brookings Institution Press.

5

Sweden's Transport Infrastructure History—Coevolution and Conflict

5.1 Transport Infrastructure Chronology 1939–2010, a Coevolutionary Perspective

The shifting influence of the different factors (technology, economics, and politics) over time on the governments role and policy formation was illustrated in Fig 3.7, and has been further developed by Hasselgren (2013a). It is argued that there has been a long-term shift from a stronger influence from technology and economics toward a policy mix with more obvious and broader influences from economics and politics. Only over the last two decades have some measures to allow other organizational forms than government ownership in transport infrastructure been discussed and partly implemented.

Over time in Sweden, there have been only a few examples where the organization and management of transport infrastructure as part of the government sector have been put into question. There seems to have been a consensus in the political system, and also among most of the business associations (confederations, chambers of commerce, motor vehicle organizations) commenting on the proposals from the numerous government committees presented over time, that the nationalized

B. Hasselgren, *Transport Infrastructure in Time, Scope and Scale*,
https://doi.org/10.1007/978-3-319-79054-1_5

system more or less functioned well. One of the main questions has instead been how to provide the system with additional financing and how to make the best use of the available resources in the systems, thus echoing a resource allocative stance, rather than a dynamic view (Fig. 5.1).

Through adjusting its ownership role and policy content over time, the government seems to have successfully accommodated the different influences from technology, economics, and politics/socioculture without opening for a more path altering discussion concerning the ownership of transport infrastructure. On a number of occasions, proposals have been put forward by the political opposition or by government committees to expand the investment plans, mainly for roads, through the introduction of tolls or other forms of alternative financing. These proposals have, however, not led to any decisions in this direction, nor have they altered the government's role in any more obvious respect.

Role of factor in the development	1939-1963	1963-1988	1989-2010
Technology (roads and railroads, rolling stock, vehicles, traffic management systems)	Strong influence	Widened use of existing technology	Growing Importance, ITS and new technology for low emission vehicles
Economics (organizational setting, scale effects, competition, transaction costs, pricing policies, marginal cost vs. full cost coverage)	Strong influence Cost responsibility and competition	Strong influence Growth of welfare economics	Strong influence Welfare economics
Politics (markets vs. government intervention, influence of other policy areas, view on distribution, local, regional, national or international)	No ideological push behind nationalization	Growing importance and broader political agenda	Strong influence Sustainability and deliberative processes
Public sector vs. Private sector	The government-managed market economy	Competition between transport modes	Preserved government ownership with some opening for alternative financing and privatization

Fig. 5.1 Transport infrastructure development chronology 1939–2010, a coevolutionary perspective (*Source* Hasselgren 2013d)

The following analysis of Swedish transport infrastructure development is organized in three time periods.

5.1.1 1939–1963—Nationalization and Professionalization

The Nationalization

Turning back to the 1930s and the processes around the nationalization of the rural public roads and the railroads in Sweden, there was a gradually growing consensus that government intervention through nationalization could be a solution to many of the perceived deficiencies of the road and railroad systems. The fast-growing road transport volumes put strong pressure on the road system. The organizations managing the rural public roads, the 170 road districts, were perceived to be lacking a professional management organization and appropriate and modern technical equipment for maintenance. The railroad system was oversized and ill structured, with a large number of local railroad corporations and different technological solutions, in addition to the National Railroad Agency. This system was in need of a restructuring in order to organize to gain from large-scale efficiencies.

According to the official documents that were presented in relation to Parliament's decisions to nationalize the rail and road systems in 1939 and 1942, there were both differences and similarities between the two decision processes (Hasselgren 2013a). The nationalization of rail can be seen as an example of a classical restructuring of an industry sector facing considerable economic difficulties due to high costs, a too fragmented structure and growing competition from the road sector.

With the fragmented organization of railroads at the time, scale economies had not been fully utilized. Government initiatives to intervene in the railroad business with grants, concessions, and loans to private railroad companies that operated independently from the government had been part of the government's policy toward the rail industry in Sweden since the 1850s. A number of railroads had been taken over by the government over the years in an ongoing centralization trend as competition from road transport became stronger. In this respect, the nationalization of railroads can be seen as logical step toward consolidation and large-scale economies. Parallel developments took place in most countries where railroad systems had been constructed during the nineteenth century. Schumpeter, in his book *Business Cycles*, argued that railroads were a business with extremely strong competition; however, following this developmental stage came a period with "consolidation, efficient administration, and sound finance" (McCraw 2007, p. 263). Consolidation was surely not just a Swedish phenomenon as discussed by Millward (2005).

Compared to railroads, roads had been part of the transportation system for some time. Roads had been built, financed, and managed by landowners (and later also by local businesses) since medieval times to enable transport in the local environment and to allow for some transport flows in wider geographical areas. Organized as an activity that local actors were responsible for, and mainly based on already present older roads, the drive in development was even less coordinated than for railroads. As such roads show many signs of a bottom-up system, rather different from railroads, with its top-down structure.

Since the 1840s, the government had been taking different coordinating measures in the road system, working for a unified system as regards financing and organization, etc. Yet, it was only during the 1920s that a more profound challenge to the local administration came. As for railroads, technology was clearly a strong driving force in the change process since the mid-nineteenth century. The numbers of cars, buses, and trucks grew fast, and transport flows developed from mainly local flows to higher proportions of regional and national flows. In 1923, national vehicle and fuel taxes were introduced, which drastically increased the government's financial resources (Liljegren 1999). By the mid-1930s, financing had become dominated by the government, and national coordinative measures had grown in importance in the early twentieth century. The government was, however, hesitating to get further involved in roads and railroads. Even if there were strong reasons based on technology, economics, and organizational aspects to take coordinative measures, according to a number of government committees analyzing these issues from the late 1800s up to the 1930s, the government refrained at length (Hasselgren 2011). A detailed report discussing the railroad nationalization (Alvfors 1977) described the debates surrounding the nationalization question during the 1920s and 1930s. This shows that opposing views as to the appropriateness of government intervention were discussed at length during the decades before the decision on the nationalization was taken.

The government's reluctance to make the final decision might partly have had to do with the political resistance against changing the basic distribution of power between the central and the regional/local levels in the public sector. There were strong opponents, mainly on the regional and local level, toward any change in the power distribution. Nationalization was believed to lead to a loss of local influence and flexibility. The risk of weakened innovativeness in a centralized railroad organization and the risk that the dynamism of the sector would be reduced were other arguments raised against the nationalization.

A parallel development can be seen in Sweden's present transport infrastructure system, as the actors are searching for new roles but where it is difficult to redistribute power in the public sector. Local governments have traditionally had a strong position in their different areas of responsibility, and the view that local responsibility should be preserved (if possible) has been widely accepted. It has generally been easier in Sweden to transfer duties to local and regional levels than to reduce their mandates, even if there have been valid arguments for centralization in different sectors over time.

The most important reason for the decision to nationalize the rural public roads seems to have been the perceived need to improve the economic performance of road management and to equalize costs between different parts of the country, more than a clear political wish for centralizing authority and power. Finally, most clearly when it comes to roads, the perceived needs of stronger government coordination in times of world crisis and war gradually seem to have influenced the decisions beside the economic reasons. The processes in relation to the nationalization of the railroads have been studied by Andersson-Skog (1993, 1996), who made similar observations. The above-mentioned studies by Bogart (2009), Clifton et al. (2011), and Millward (2005, 2011) point in similar directions concerning nationalization in other Western countries.

There might also have been some interdependence between the two decisions: When the resistance toward nationalization of railroads was overcome in 1939, it might have been easier to go ahead with road nationalization in 1942. Still, the general impression is that the government waited a long time to make the final decisions, and, when it did, it was based more on pragmatism and economic rationality than on ideology or politics. The government shows signs of only reluctantly having to take on the responsibility for the wider transport infrastructure systems.

The political or sociocultural system at the local and regional levels was largely in favor of preserving the existing system more than for reform. The decision to organize transport infrastructure as part of the existing government agencies was at the same time consistent with the government's intention to foster coordination and economizing policies both for railroads and roads. Other organizational models, such as state-owned corporations, could, of course, have been discussed, but they did not appear in the discussion, even if Alvfors (1977) points to the fact that a private sector restructuring alternative for railroads had been discussed at length up to the nationalization decision (Fig. 5.2).

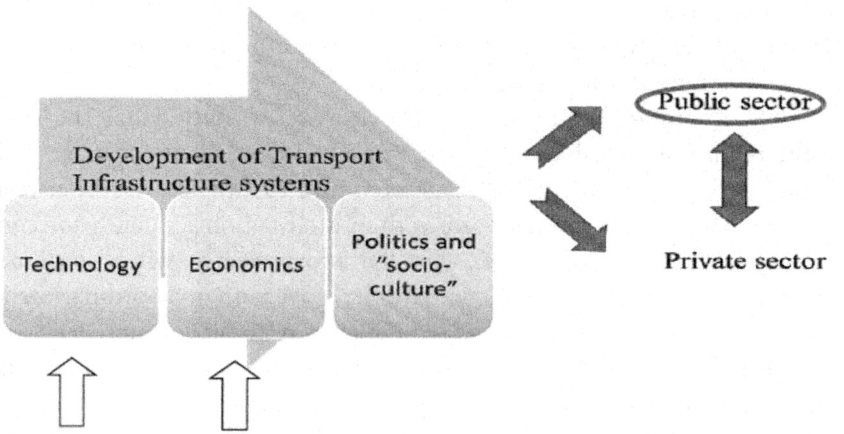

Fig. 5.2 An influence from technology and economic factors explain the nationalization

Policy Formation Following the Second World War

Since the nationalization, the influence of technological, economic, and political factors on the government's formation of its transport infrastructure policies and its ownership role have varied. For transport policy and transport infrastructure development, the period from 1945 to 1963, when the first major decision on transport policy was taken following the Second World War, is in many ways a history of the growing importance of the road transport system and the contracting railroad system. A main focus of the policy area, and for the government's ownership role, was how to frame the development of the road transport system in terms of a developed road planning system and coherent financing principles. For the railroad system, the main focus was instead how to finance the growing deficits, which was an effect of the competition from road transport. The Railroad Administration was focused on reducing the railroad system or lobbying to increase government support for those parts of the railroads that were unprofitable. From around the 1920s onward, the railroad system in this respect resembles the role of a "reverse salient" (Hughes 1987) in the transport system, representing the part of the system that was lagging behind from a technological point of view and that demanded financial support from the political system. At the same time, the road system had positive momentum with a strong growth and a number of supporting actors, such as consumers and producers of vehicles, and supporting services and the road lobby organizations (Blomkvist 2001).

In terms of the coevolutionary perspective, the development during this period seems to have been influenced by technology in terms of the strengthening of the motor transport technology. Economic factors were though even more important since there was a push to set a financing framework for the road network and in general to foster efficiency, with the application of the *cost responsibility principle*. This principle meant that the road and railroad sectors should cover their full financial costs with fees and taxes collected from the respective users of the systems. This principle, which had its origin in an earlier period in transport infrastructure policies, had an important role in limiting the growth of the investments in the sector.

> A dynamic development is rarely centrally planned. It grows as a product of, among other things, imagination and impulses among a multitude of business-men, who in mutual competition with varying success experiment without being prevented by anything than necessary regulations. Administrative dirigisme, implemented by ever so skilled public officers, will on the contrary inevitably largely build upon the present state. Dirigisme thus, in general, has a preservative effect. (The 1944 Transport Committee, SOU 1947:85, pp. 52–53)

With regard to the balance between public- and private-sector provision, the policy, within a framework of government ownership, was relatively market-oriented, focusing on full cost coverage with positive values connected to entrepreneurial activity and competition between transport modes. The 1944 Transport Committee, as exemplified by the excerpt above, expressed a view on transport policy that was close to a stance inspired by Schumpeter and Hayek (Fig. 5.3).

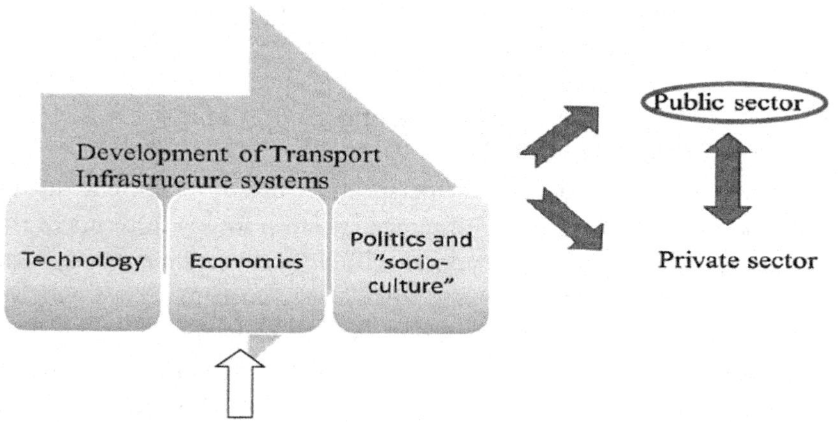

Fig. 5.3 Postwar transport policies were influenced by available resources in relation to demand for new roads

5.1.2 1963–1988 and 1989—The Present—Social Marginal Costs or Not?

The period of 1963–1980 was characterized by a prolongation of the postwar policies based on competition between the transport modes, but also with an increasing openness to welfare economics as a guiding framework and as part of this social cost–benefit analysis. As a balance to this fairly market-oriented decentralized policy stance, a centralized expert orientation was seen as the modern way of handling societal planning in, for example, road-sector planning (Hultén 2012).

A growing criticism toward the expert orientation of the planning system and the perceived road transport-friendly stance of the infrastructure policies during the 1960s led to a gradual reorientation of the policies. This also coincided with the successively developed use of cost–benefit analysis, in which wider political goals could be implemented in a formal structure.

> ... the welfare economic objective has to be the basis for the continued development of transport policy.
>
> ---
>
> The transport system has to be coordinated through an appropriate and continuous public sector traffic planning... consistent with guidelines... set by the government. (Transport 1975 Policy Committee, SOU 1975:66, p. 44)

From the 1980s, there has been a stronger political influence over transport policy combined with market openings and deregulation. The shift as regards the basic view on transport policy is exemplified by the 1975 Transport Policy Committee excerpt above. Deliberative influences have been strengthened in physical and economic planning, as well as in the operations of the Road and Railroad Administrations, with cost–benefit analysis and a marked process orientation in both planning and operation of the systems as important signs. Thoresson (2011) makes a similar remark in a recent study into the use of cost–benefit analysis in transport planning. According to this study, the political influence has increased in the sector and cost–benefit analysis has been strengthened following the transport policy decision taken by Parliament in 1998.

This decision was more openly political compared to earlier decisions on transport infrastructure.

During the same time period, there has been a period when alternatives to government ownership and financing have been realized, for example, privatization of some parts of the former Road and Rail Administrations' operations. In addition, more efficient procurement methods have been introduced, and larger portions of the Administrations' construction and maintenance operations have gradually been transferred to external suppliers. Today, the Transport Administration has only limited in-house resources for maintenance and construction work.

Even if a general user charge system has not been a solution to the perceived need for additional financing of roads, measures have been implemented through which the use of government borrowing for financing of investments as an alternative to appropriations has been made possible. Congestion charging and lately some examples of user fees are other examples of a more open policy to these measures over the last 10–15 years. Deregulation of rail transport with market openings for competition has also been a measure during this period, at first for freight transport and recently for rail passenger transport. The political system has thus been working for strengthened political goal orientation, while at the same time opening for alternatives to government's ownership of railroads and roads.

Sweden's entry into the EU in 1995 not only brought a higher degree of internationalization, but also supported the reorganization of the transport markets and transport infrastructure agencies in Sweden initiated in the 1980s. Part of the EU policy in this sector is to initiate stronger competition through liberalization and the opening up of national transport markets. Recently, at the EU level, there is openness to private-sector initiatives, partly as a result of weak public finances following the financial crisis from 2008 to 2012. Through different measures designed for supporting private-sector initiatives, such as PPPs participation, the European Commission has strived for higher efficiency in the EU's measures and looked to boost available resources.

However, after a wide-ranging analysis of the EU's consolidated strategies on Trans-European Networks (TENs), Johnson and Turner (2007) note that the market-friendly liberal strategy of the 1980–1990s in many EU countries to some extent has been altered to lean more on the traditional incumbents, for example, when it comes to the spread of new technology or interoperability in different subsectors such as transport. In Sweden, as in many other countries, criticism toward privatization and PPPs has recently been voiced, partly as a response to the effects of the financial crisis (Fig. 5.4).

Technology has also regained some of its former influence during the last decade. Intelligent Transport Systems (ITSs) with IT-based solutions have become more important for traffic management and control. Sustainability aspects of transport have also strengthened the focus on technology development of new vehicles, for example. Furthermore, new payment systems have become alternatives to tax financing, with congestion taxes and charges for capacity utilization for train operators as examples.

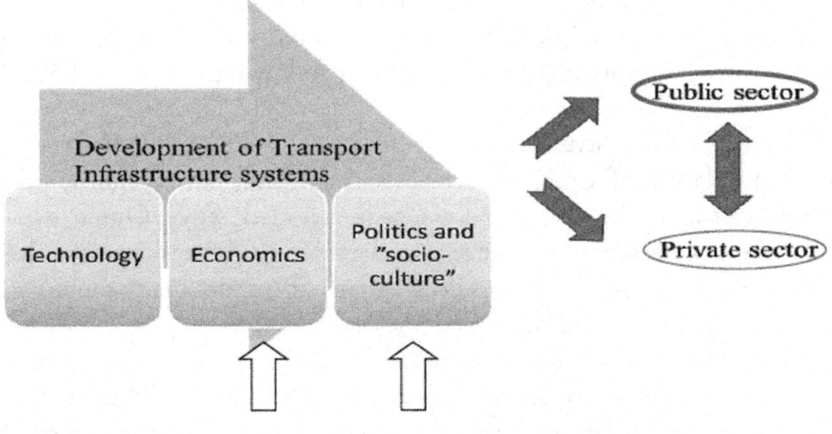

Fig. 5.4 Since the 1970s welfare economics and politics have increasingly influenced transport infrastructure policies

5.1.3 Conclusions

This section has outlined that the coevolutionary approach gives an understanding and analysis of the development of transport infrastructure and the government's role from the 1930s to the 2010s.

The different factors in the model have had varying impacts during the period and affected policy decisions in different ways. The government seems to have been reluctant to engage itself as owner of the road and railroad systems and waited a long time to take these measures. As owner of the systems, the government has acted pragmatically and through gradual policy development and adjustment preserved its ownership of roads and railroads.

5.2 Marginal Cost Controversies—Different Views on Financing

5.2.1 Financing Principles

There are two different principles based on which assets like transport infrastructure could be priced: marginal cost coverage and full cost coverage. These two principles have varied in importance and influence in the Swedish transport infrastructure sector following the Second World War.

Over time, successive investments in roads and railroads have led to the accumulation of a major asset base which, from an economic point of view, can be treated as sunk costs, as mentioned above. One reason is that even if the assets represent a considerable value they have few alternative uses. The cost of tearing down roads and railroads if there is no future transport need is also considerable.

The operation and maintenance of assets like pavement, platforms, and signal systems are necessary for the use of roads and railroads; however, use leads to wear and tear of the assets. Combined these costs are more or less equivalent to the short-term marginal costs. This situation is a sound economic basis for charging users of the present road and railroad systems only for these marginal costs.

If the depreciation of the current systems, as well as investment costs for reconstruction and new construction of roads and railroads are also considered, the cost basis is of course considerably much wider than what is represented by short-term marginal costs. In a system where all of these wider costs are covered, a full cost coverage concept is in use. Furthermore, if the external costs of the system, such as noise and air pollution, are taken into account, a short-term (or long-term if so chosen) social marginal cost measure and cost coverage concept are at hand. As will be exemplified below, these theoretical measures have been part of the policy discussions on transport infrastructure in Sweden.

5.2.2 A Government Dilemma and Coase's View

As the decisions to nationalize the road and railroad systems had been taken in Sweden by the late 1930s and early 1940s, the government had to decide on the future financing policies for roads and railroads and how to charge the users. The above-mentioned financing principles of marginal or full cost coverage were a major part of the discussions around the financing policies in Sweden.

The starting point was a situation where both the road and railroad systems were in need of considerable investments. Not only had investments been low during the Second World War, but transport flows also increased rapidly during the 1940s and 1950s. The government intended to both strengthen the infrastructure systems and preserve the macroeconomic stability, which was seen as threatened by too high demand aggregated over the war years for import of goods and investments in the domestic sectors. This situation made a discussion on how to finance the transport infrastructure system necessary.

Similar discussions were taking place in other European countries where large domestic industries, utilities, and infrastructure assets had been nationalized. In Britain, this discussion was brought to the forefront in a series of articles by Coase (1946, 1947) discussing the pricing principles for utilities and exemplified by railroads. The first of the articles was titled Marginal Cost Controversies.

Nationalization of transport infrastructure widened the scope for marginal cost-based pricing and also opened for more government redistribution and subsidies. This view had been fostered by the prominent British economist Pigou, who argued for government intervention and subsidies to industries where a spontaneous market organization might lead to monopolistic tendencies and loss of consumer surplus. Coase argued that many of the theoretical ideas, such as Pigou's, were lacking a full analysis of organizational and incentive problems and aspects. There was thus a pressing need to discuss these issues from a theoretical point of view.

Coase's (1946) article was based on the view that the spontaneous interaction of single actors in the economy has a much wider potential of leading to efficient solutions than the neoclassical welfare-inspired economists generally argued. Coase was reluctant to accept that the government could be in a position to access the knowledge necessary in order to correctly estimate the individual actors' demand. Coase argued that the government would not be able to mirror the allocation of resources between different purposes that a system with prices reflecting the full resource-use would bring.

Another point of criticism was that only resource allocation based on prices reflecting the full cost would foster social learning. According to Coase (1946, p. 176), in a situation where new investments were planned, the information inherited from the experiences of the viability of past investments, which have been put to the test of the market, should also be taken into account. In the case of organizations operating under marginal cost pricing, this information would not be available. Estimation, and here Coase quotes Hotelling, must be carried out facing "not a historical, but a mathematical and economic problem" (p. 175). Experience based on learning in Coase's model was contrasted against a deductive calculative method forwarded by welfare economics, which becomes more or less a necessity when following that view. When accessing the texts today, it is also apparent that Hotelling was adhering to a rather formalistic approach, while Coase was primarily stating his case backed by a general organizational discourse.

The argumentation from the two sides echoed to some degree the disputes between Keynes and Hayek during the 1930s, where Keynes worked at a macro-level and recommended government intervention as a remedy against lacking demand in the economy and unemployment, while Hayek argued for an understanding of investment and business behavior at a more individual level (Bas 2011). The disputes from the 1930s around these issues were still at hand as the government formulated a financing principle. As for incentives, Coase's argument was that markets without government intervention, where corporations are pricing the services to cover full costs, must be preferred to a controlled market situation, where the government in some way administers the prices. One of the reasons for this view was that there was a risk for overinvestment in transport infrastructure, which Coase suggested as one of the deficiencies with marginal cost pricing, as discussed earlier.

Coase's arguments against marginal cost-based pricing (without full cost coverage) are condensed into the following arguments:

- Marginal cost pricing would lead to maldistribution of the production factors, since the full costs of these would not be obvious to the user.
- Marginal cost pricing would lead to income distribution from nonusers to users and from taxpayers to users.
- Marginal cost pricing, if combined with tax subsidies, would lead to "other harmful effects" as the economy is more heavily tax-burdened.
- Marginal cost pricing would lead to a risk of overconsumption and lack of information on how to spend resources in the future, since price signals are distorted.

Coase presented four arguments in favor of an alternative pricing system based on multipart pricing, with separate payments to cover fixed and variable costs. With such a system, the user would face the full cost of the resources that are used for the production of the good or service, which would confer a correct combined price signal. Besides the view that tax financing would lead to decreased allocative efficiency in the economy in general, Coase presented a number of arguments focusing on the positive effects of markets and the relation between customers and suppliers offering services at full price. It safeguards correct allocation of resources, learning, and an incentive structure that gives a good basis for efficient management and operations of the supplying organizations. Coase's discussion emphasizes the situation of the producing organization and its relation to users or customers. This organizational view can be traced back to Coase's 1937 article The Nature of the Firm, where he discussed the arguments in favor of organizations in a world of loose relationships that often defines markets.

Coase returned to this discussion in a later article (Coase 1970), arguing that the financing principle affects the organization of the businesses to a great extent. He argued that government subsidies, which is generally an integral part of the marginal cost-based pricing principle, would eventually lead to centralization to the government, as it would naturally be interested in controlling the organization it subsidizes. Coase argued that "some financial autonomy is a necessary aspect of efficient administration." This would indicate that a policy of marginal cost pricing "would be very bad because it would lead in the end to a complete centralization of the administration of public utilities." (p. 119).

The different perspectives are summarized in Fig. 5.5. The horizontal axis represents the spectrum between marginal cost coverage and full cost coverage. On the vertical axis, the dichotomy between earmarking (all revenues are directly allocated to the supplier) and the treatment of user payments as general tax revenues is displayed. Coase's model which is placed in the upper left corner combines full cost coverage with earmarking (which is not explicitly stated by Coase but might be assumed from the general reasoning in the articles where the discussed positive incentive effects connected to full cost coverage signal a financing principle close to earmarking). The Pigovian welfare economics model, also represented by scholars as Hotelling, is displayed in the lower right corner, which combines marginal cost coverage with the treatment of revenues from taxes and fees as general tax income.

Lindsey (2006), going through the later development of economists' views on road pricing up to the 2000s, notes that the more institutional sentiment that Coase represents has not been the core element of economists' handling of issues on road pricing in general (p. 315).

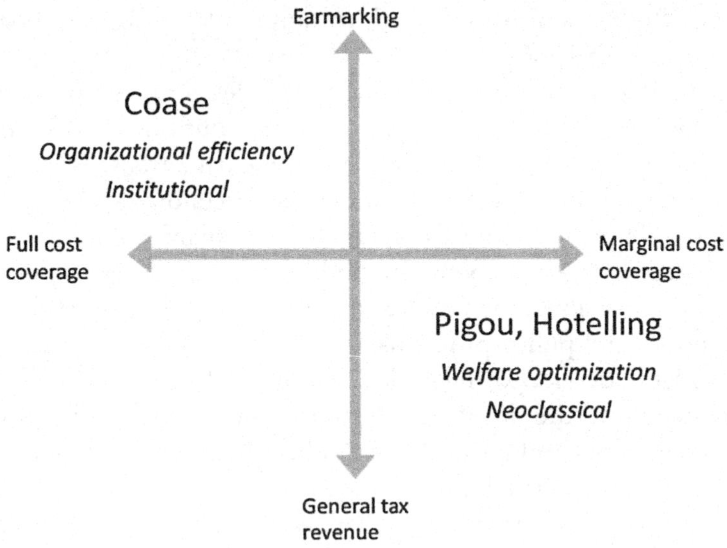

Fig. 5.5 Coase and Pigou/Hotelling—different views on cost coverage and financing

The view represented by Pigou has, since the 1940s, instead largely been dominant and further developed by a number of scholars such as Vickrey, Walters, and Mohring. Pricing of road use based on short-term (social) marginal cost has been the basis for these later scholars' writing. Small, Winston, and Evans, among others, according to Lindsey, have shown that under some assumptions congestion and road damage charges can pay for the costs of both capacity and maintenance (p. 312). This line of theorizing has also been possible to express in mathematics and in graphical form, which has probably added to the strength of this view among economists, and also to its impact on the public discussion of the pricing issues.

The institutional view, which was exemplified by road and railroad, and related themes in Coase's 1940s articles have, according to Lindsey, not been widely developed with further applications in this sector of the economy. As an exception, the writings of Gabriel Roth can be mentioned. Roth (2006) has edited one of the later works where a number of articles discuss the prospects and favors of a more privatized road provision. Roth has also published a number of articles and books in this field since the 1960s.

In another overview article covering the development of transportation economics through the last 30 years, Button (2010) presents a more or less similar view of the development of transportation economics. Even if a microeconomic and welfare economics view in transport economics has been developed in the dominant tradition, Button, though, seems to worry about the high abstraction level in microeconomic transportation economics and, thus, the fairly low relevance to actual politics and policy problems. There is a frustration in this article that the highly developed theoretical models and analyses do not really make its way into the decisions. Button points to the need to include institutional theory and insights from political economy into the discussion in order to raise its relevance for policy.

A similar approach is presented by Winston (2010), who suggests privatization experiments be introduced as a means for addressing many of the problems of the US transportation system such as lack of innovativeness and resources and slow productivity growth. The institutional view is obviously represented by contemporary scholars, even if the welfare or neoclassical bias is generally the stronger in discussions around transport infrastructure.

While Coase favored a system where roads and railroads were financed without government subsidies, the more recent institutional studies mentioned above seem mostly focused on an improvement and methodological refinement of the application of short-term social marginal cost-based financing models. By reducing cross-subsidies between different transport modes and striving for price setting that is more in line with real-life marginal costs (including, e.g., congestion induced costs), a higher level of efficiency could, according to this view, be achieved than in many present systems.

This seems to be a view where a move from weaker to more powerful incentives is sought after, while not necessarily meeting the requirements of Coase, aiming for full cost coverage. Even if short-term social marginal cost pricing could be expected to raise sufficient resources to cover the full costs of roads in urban congested areas, this would clearly not be the case in less populated areas. There would thus still be a need for substantial tax financing and cross-subsidization if these pricing models were fully applied. This is of course something that is even truer with regard to railroads, where marginal cost style user charges often only cover even lesser parts of the total costs than for roads.

5.2.3 A Marginal Cost Controversy in Swedish Transport Infrastructure Policy?

At least at the official policy level, which is the focus here, the discussion in Sweden around pricing and financing policies related to transport infrastructure can be seen as a controversy between the two different perspectives, as outlined by Coase in his 1946 and 1947 articles. The controversy seems to have been strongest during the 1970–1980s, when a shift from a cost-responsibility principle to a social marginal cost principle was discussed at length in the official documents in relation to transport infrastructure policy. Since that time, the social marginal cost principle has been the dominant official policy, though often blended with more business economic-inspired contents. This development has been underpinned by EU policies, where the same blend of marginal cost and full cost pricing policy is also apparent.

This process of gradual change from the full cost coverage policy to the marginal cost policy is described in more detail in two articles (Hasselgren 2013b, c). Three periods are described in the articles during which different financing policies were followed. These coincide relatively well with the time periods used in the discussion above on the formation of general policies in the transport infrastructure sector. The three periods discussed with regard to the financing principles are:

- 1944–1978 The Full Cost Coverage Period
- 1979–1988 The Mixed Policies Period
- 1989–2010 The Social Marginal Cost Period.

The period from 1944 until 1978 was marked by a policy that aimed for full cost coverage for each of the transport modes on a stand-alone basis. This principle was more or less strictly upheld during different time periods within the broader period, with a subsequent softening during the late 1960s or 1970s. In 1979, a new principle was set by the government based on welfare economics principles. The current or existing investments in roads and railroads should be seen as sunk costs, and only short-term social marginal costs should be the basis for pricing and taxation.

Not until the late 1980s or early 1990s has a clearer move from this principle been implemented. As from 1979 when the formal policies were changed to a marginal cost model, these eventually turned out not to have been fully implemented. Then in 1988, the government decided that the decision in 1979 had gone too far and therefore made something of a compromise, bringing back some of the former principles with cost coverage and per-mode focus for financing into the official policies.

However, during the 1990s, the short-term social marginal cost principle has gradually become more important, partly as a result of the split of the former Railroad Agency in operations and infrastructure as separate organizations. The merger of the former Rail Administration and the Road Administration in 2010 was also a sign of the government's intention to foster a multimodal perspective in transport policy and transport infrastructure policy in general, a principle taking financing even further away from earmarking and a cost-responsibility view.

5.2.4 Reasons for the Change in Policies

The change in the financing principles that occurred gradually from the nationalization until the early 2000s can be seen as inspired or caused by a number of arguments and the general political development.

As Sannerstedt (1979) has shown, there was widespread criticism toward the reduction in the railroad system in the public Swedish debate in the 1960s, following the 1963 transport policy decision. The parallel growth of road transport and the planning and construction program for roads was met with concerns over the perceived technocratic expert stance of the planning system. A general critique was that a single-handed focus on roads and car transport would lead to a society and urban development that was not desirable. The critical standpoints were reflected in a debate book by a group of academics (Anell et al. 1971) critically discussing the effects of the expansion of the road system and arguing for a revised transport policy. One main point in the book was the perceived overly road transport-friendly stance of Swedish transport policy.

Another key element of the critique was that road traffic in general did not pay for its full social cost, specifically claiming that negative externalities were not included in the calculations of the cost base that should be covered by tax and fees. Railroads, on the other hand, it was argued, had to pay their full costs, which rendered them at a competitive disadvantageous situation in relation to road traffic. The authors here almost argued for reversing the financing principle of the time, from alleged marginal to full cost for roads and from likewise alleged full cost to marginal cost coverage for railroads.

Another critical standpoint was raised by Bohm, a well-known Swedish economist at the time active in transport economics. Bohm argued that the government's 1972 Road Tax Committee was heading for the right principles of the future: short-term social marginal costs as the basis for pricing decisions (Bohm 1973). The ministry officials and the prevailing transport policy could though, according to Bohm, be expected to work for a too strong focus on the principle of full cost coverage and "the single sided focus on business economic efficiency" (p. 326), which was the basis of the 1963 transport policy decision.

Bohm presented a number of articles and books at this time that argued for a stronger role for welfare economics principles in transport infrastructure planning and financing discussions. In 1974, Bohm et al. published a general and comprehensive critique of the 1963 transport policy and its effects. Here, the critical voices of the late 1960s and early 1970s, those specifically against road planning and further road construction, were the starting point of the discussion. It was argued that through a wider use of cost–benefit analysis and welfare economics principles a redirection of the transport policy that focused more on welfare-based efficiency should be achieved.

Welfare economics-based theory, besides being theoretically backed, seems also to have allowed for more active policy and government intervention, which could be a political solution to the new situation with stronger political concerns voiced in the debate around transport policy. The fiscal interest in revenues from road transport-related taxes, which increased over time, might also have made the earlier strict connection between revenues and government appropriations less favored from a fiscal policy (Ministry of Finance) perspective. The income surplus from these taxes could be used for other purposes in a situation with growing public financing of different activities not only within the sector, for example, coverage of growing deficits in railroads, but also in other sectors.

The academic support for a shift to welfare economics-inspired cost–benefit calculation, as a basis for prioritization in decisions on transport infrastructure spending, also seems to have fit well into a political system looking for a way to formalize the stronger interest in communicative planning processes for roads and railroads. Through the introduction of cost–benefit analysis, there was a method for including external variables into the discussion without losing too much of the rationalist stance of earlier government infrastructure planning practices. Deliberative planning processes and formal cost–benefit calculations were methods that worked well together.

The government's interest in a more elaborated and wider scope for transport policy in order to include regional policy concerns, environmental concerns, and more active industrial and physical planning policies also made cost–benefit calculation a helpful tool. The further development of cost–benefit analysis can be seen as a method for introducing these new policy goals other than production economics or business economics, which had been the stronger of the goals in the sector since the 1940s. Hultén (2012) and Thoresson (2011) make similar observations when discussing the Swedish transport infrastructure planning system. Cost–benefit analysis has developed into a method used to include different perspectives in the planning process.

At the same time, the historical record from the 1940s to the 2010s as reflected on in the articles by Hasselgren mentioned above shows that the government has been pragmatic when formulating its policies compared to the government committees' proposals. When the proposed policies from the 1940 to 1960s leaned toward deregulation and markets, the government was somewhat slower to deregulate and supported railroads more than the official policy should perhaps have prescribed. As the social marginal cost policy was introduced, the government had been fostering administrative efforts to increase efficiency and allowed for user funding for specific projects. The government then seems to have played a pragmatic role in the system by balancing different needs and goals.

5.2.5 Incentives for Efficiency Changed?

Another possible way to express the change in the government's principles for financing might be that there has been a shift in focus of the discussion from a view close to Coase's standpoint in the 1940s, where the efficient operation of the road and railroad agencies was an important concern for the government and government committees analyzing the policy area. The present focus, which has grown stronger since the 1970s, has rather been that maximization of welfare surplus should be the overriding goal of the government's policies, and only second comes the interest for organizational efficiency. This shift in the policy stance is presented in Fig. 5.6.

The shift might be interpreted as a departure from the focus on the internal efficiency of the producing organizations and their relation to the users to a focus on the external efficiency. These wider relations between the transport infrastructure system and the surrounding economy are seen as not being reflected in the narrower decisions on costs and income generated internally in the infrastructure system. The two concepts, *internal* and *external* efficiency, were used by government committees in the 1970s and 1980s, as these discussed the different efficiency concepts and the perspectives that should be favored.

As Fig. 5.6 shows, this change in focus has also been combined with a policy reorientation from a principle of earmarking the government's revenues from (primarily) road transport used for road maintenance and investments to a model wherein government revenues are treated as general tax revenues used at the discretion of Parliament and government in yearly budget decisions. The former principle reflects a view that there

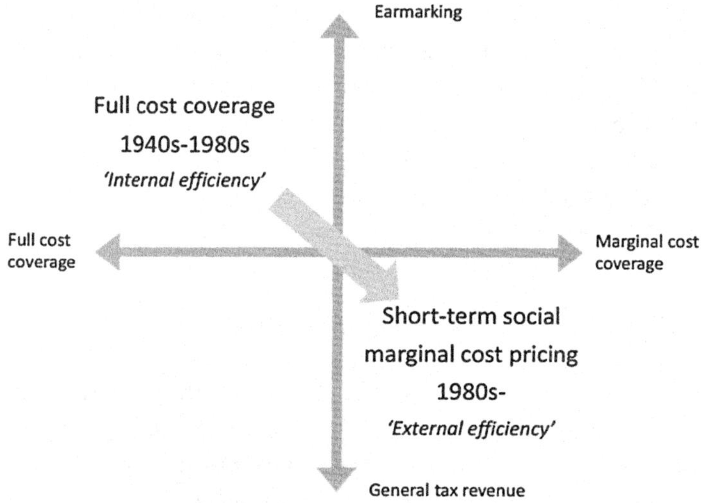

Fig. 5.6 The marginal cost controversy in Sweden's transport infrastructure policy

should be a connection between revenues and actual spending in the same sector, perhaps a parallel to the Wicksellian interest principle for taxation. The latter principle comes closer to a theoretical public finance view, where all decisions on government spending should be taken as a comprehensive package and all available revenues are reflected against all spending purposes. This latter principle is also reflected in fiscal regulation frameworks in Sweden.

Only a few exceptions of this overriding rule have been allowed, for example, for some major bridges and for revenues from road congestions charging and railroad user charges. The incentive effects connected to the different pricing principles were discussed in a number of reports issued by government committees from the 1940 to 1990s, as shown in the appended articles. However, the focus of these questions has become less marked over time. The initial post-Second World War discussion was clear in this respect: The government was seen to have a role in fostering good management and organizations. Later discussions on these matters have been less developed and less explicit.

The shift from stronger to weaker incentives for organizational efficiency seems to have been combined with growing subsidies from the government to the railroads and with stronger fiscal interests expressed by the government as a motivation for road transport taxation. Revenues from fuel-based taxes have grown gradually, as VAT on top of the gasoline price including taxes was introduced in Sweden in the early 1990s. However, recently there has been some decline in the gross tax income related to fuel (Ekonomistyrningsverket 2013), which might be connected to the successive introduction of more fuel-efficient vehicles. If Coase's cautions toward policies of this kind should be listened to, we should expect the overall efficiency of the operations of the systems and the general allocation of resources in the economy to have become less efficient as the incentives fostering productivity and efficiency have become weaker.

The change from general tax revenue funding to fee funding, in a system where government agencies operate the systems, might be a step to strengthen incentives working for customer focus and internal efficiency. There would, however, still be difficulties connected to the government model such as weak incentives for customer orientation and the risk that government agencies would prioritize internal aims in the organization more than the official policy (Wagner 1991/2011). One additional observation is that the government has gradually emphasized a market failure view with regard to its view on the functioning of the transport infrastructure system. Compared to the more openly positive market economy-friendly view expressed by the 1944 Transport Committee, this is a major change.

References

Alvfors, K.-G. (1977). *Järnvägsförstatligandet - svensk järnvägspolitik under 1930-talet.* Svenska järnvägsklubbens skriftserie nr 21.

Andersson-Skog, L. (1993). *Såsom allmänna inrättningar till gagnet, men affärsföretag till namnet. SJ, järnvägspolitiken och den ekonomiska omvandlingen efter 1920*, Aa Umeå.

Andersson-Skog, L. (1996). From State Railway Housekeeping to Railway Economics, Swedish Railway Policy and Economic Transformation After 1920 in an Institutional Perspective. *Scandinavian Economic History Review, 44*(1), 23–42.

Anell, L., Hedborg, A., Lönnroth, M., & Ingelstam, L. (1971). *Ska vi asfaltera Sverige?* Stockholm: Pan/Norstedts.

Bas, D. S. (2011). Hayek's Critique of the General Theory: A New View of the Debate Between Hayek and Keynes. *The Quarterly Journal of Austrian Economics, 14*(3), 288–310.

Blomkvist, P. (2001). *Den goda vägens vänner – Väg- och billobbyn och framväxten av det svenska bilsamhället 1914–1959.* Stockholm/Stehag: Brutus Östlings Bokförlag Symposion.

Bogart, D. (2009). Nationalizations and the Development of Transport Systems: Cross-Country Evidence from Railroad Ne tworks, 1860–1912. *The Journal of Economic History, 69*(01), 202–237.

Bohm, P. (1973). Ansvarigt och oansvarigt om bilismens kostnader. *Ekonomisk Debatt, 1*(5), 326–330. Stockholm.

Bohm, P., Bruzelius, N., Hesselborn, P.-O., Johannesson, M., Ruud, T., & Thedéen, T. (1974). *Transportpolitiken och samhällsekonomin.* Stockholm: LiberFörlag.

Button, K. (2010). Transportation Economics: Some Developments Over the Past 30 Years. *Journal of the Transportation Research Forum, 45*(2), 7–30.

Clifton, J., Lanthier, P., & Schröter, H. (2011). Regulating and Deregulating the Public Utilities 1830–2010. *Business History, 53*(5), 659–672.

Coase, R. H. (1946). The Marginal Cost Controversy. *Economica*, New Series, *13*(51), 169–182.

Coase, R. H. (1947). The Marginal Cost Controversy: Some Further Comments. *Economica*, New Series, *14*(54), 150–153.

Coase, R. H. (1970). The Theory of Public Utility Pricing and Its Application. *The Bell Journal of Economics and Management Science, 1*(1), 113–128.

Ekonomistyrningsverket. (2013). Utfallet för statens budget – del av ESVs underlag för årsredovisning för staten 2012, ESV 2013:23, Stockholm.

Hasselgren, B. (2011). *The Reluctant Infrastructure Manager: Nationalization of Rail and Road Infrastructure in Sweden, 1930 to 1940.* Presented at Transportation Research Board's Annual Meeting 2012, USA.

Hasselgren, B. (2013a). The Swedish Government as Owner of Transport Infrastructure. Policy Formation from the 1930s to the 2010s. *Scandinavian Journal of Public Administration, 16*(4), 49–71.

Hasselgren, B. (2013b). Pricing Principles, Efficiency Concepts and Incentive Models in Swedish Transport Infrastructure Policy, Reprinted from VTI Rapport 787, pp. 22–35, Swedish National Road and Transport Research Institute (VTI), Linköping.

Hasselgren, B. (2013c). Marginal Cost Controversies in Swedish Transport Infrastructure Policy. Aalborg University, Denmark.

Hasselgren, B. (2013d). Pricing Principles, Efficiency Concepts and Incentive Models in Swedish Transport Infrastructure Policy, Reprinted from VTI rapport 787, pp. 22–35, Swedish National Road and Transport Research Institute (VTI), Linköping.

Hughes, T. P. (1987). Reverse Salients and Critical Problems: The Dynamics of Technological Change. In G. Dosi, R. Giannetti, & P. A. Toninelli (Eds.), *Technology and enterprise in a historical perspective*, 97–118. Oxford: Clarendon Press.

Hultén, J. (2012). Nya vägar till järnvägar och vägar, Finansieringspragmatism och planeringsrationalism vid beslut om infrastrukturinvesteringar, *Political Studies* 166. Lund.

Johnson, D., & Turner, C. (2007). *Strategy and Policy for Trans-European Networks*. Houndmills, Basingstoke, Hampshire: Palgrave Macmillan.

Liljegren, E. (1999). *Den stora förvirringen. Partipolitik och bilintressen i riksdagsbehandlingen av bilskatternas utformning 1922–1939* (Working Papers in Transport and Communication History No. 1999:5). Sweden: Umeå University and Uppsala University.

Lindsey, R. (2006). Do Economists Reach a Conclusion on Road Pricing? The Intellectual History of an Idea. *Economic Journal Watch, 3*(2), 292–379.

McCraw, T. K. (2007). *Prophet of Innovation, Joseph Schumpeter and Creative Destruction*. Cambridge, MA and London, UK: Belknap Press of Harvard University Press.

Millward, R. (2005). *Private and Public Enterprise in Europe*. UK: Cambridge University Press.

Millward, R. (2011). Public Enterprise in the Modern Western World: An Historical Analysis. *Annals of Public and Cooperative Economics, 82*(4), 378–398.

Roth, G. (Ed.). (2006). *Street Smart, Competition, Entrepreneurship and the Future of Roads*. The Independent Institute, Transaction Publishers.

Sannerstedt, A. (1979). *Fri konkurrens eller politisk styrning? 1963 års trafikpolitiska beslut – debatten om innehåll, tillämpning och effekter*. Studentlitteratur: Lund: Studentlitteratur.

SOU 1947:85 "Det inrikes trafikväsendet", 1944-års trafikpolitiska utredning, Stockholm.

SOU 1975:66 Transport Policy Committee, Stockholm.

Thoresson, K. (2011). *Att beräkna det goda samhället: Samhällsekonomiska analyser och gränslandet expertis-politik inom transportområdet* (Doctoral Dissertation, Linköping.

Wagner, R. E. (Ed.). (1991/2011). *Charging for Government: User Charges and Earmarked Taxes in Principle and Practice*. New York, USA: Routledge Revivals.

Winston, C. (2010). *Last Exit – Privatization and Deregulation of the U.S. Transportation System*. Washington, DC: Brookings Institution Press.

Concluding Remarks

To conclude transport infrastructure develops over time, space and scale in patterns that seem to revolve over time. Shifts between organizations in the public sector and by private sector actors are a recurring theme. As the scale and scope of transport infrastructure changes it is also the case that ownership-control and financing (and planning) takes new forms but mostly in waves between centralization/governmentalization as altered by decentralization/privatization. Over time there is an alternative to strategic infrastructure planning, that is being organized as public-sector activities (only).

Openings for decentralized spontaneous market orderings is an alternative that has been discussed in the literature and of which there are numerous examples in reality, based on proprietary rights. These alternatives seem to offer a variety of local solutions and learning processes at many different levels in society. Ideas and themes from the discussion on multi-level governance seem to come close to these alternatives. The knowledge problem, which is inherent in centralized decision structures, perhaps particularly in the public sector, also seems likely to handle with measures like these to some extent. Reforms within the public sector primarily focused on reorganization at new spatial levels might

B. Hasselgren, *Transport Infrastructure in Time, Scope and Scale*,
https://doi.org/10.1007/978-3-319-79054-1

though, without an understanding of the planning potentials at different spatial levels, result in new government failures.

The two current different development strategies in the EU and the US seem primarily to represent the public-sector variants of centralization and decentralization. Some measures conforming to market practices are apparent but could probably be strengthened compared to the present policies.

The success of actually having the Interstate Highway System in the US built was partly due to the stronger coordination powers that the federal government was given in the 1950s. Without arguing that all the decisions taken in relation to this system were necessarily justified or well informed from a coordination and knowledge perspective, it seems likely that the centralization of powers during this period was decisive for the success of the construction program. This could be a message to the EU in the current situation. Stronger strategic coordination might be called for if missing links in the EU transport infrastructure system should be realized. Another important message from the point of view might be that market orderings, to the extent possible, should be utilized. These orderings seem to produce knowledge as an end result. Strategic transport infrastructure planning could possibly favor a combination of both measures.

Mainstream literature, while partly discussing institutional aspects on transport infrastructure planning and acknowledging information and agency-related phenomena, seems surprisingly disconnected from the discussion around how coordination in the economy actually can arise. This is true also for the limited (at least explicit) interest in the knowledge problem in public sector planning. All in all, the perspectives of time, scope, and scale tells us something additional about transport infrastructure in comparison to the main stream paradigms of neoclassical and centralized government responsibility for transport infrastructure systems. It is important that we continue to learn more about these alternative perspectives in order to understand transport infrastructure and its development over time.

References

Government Committees and Government Bills

SOU 1947:85 "Det inrikes trafikväsendet", 1944-års trafikpolitiska utredning, Stockholm.

SOU 1975:66 Transport Policy Committee, Stockholm.

SOU 2011:49 "Medfinansiering av transportinfrastruktur", Stockholm.

Bill 2008/09:31 Transportstyrelsen och dess verksamhet, Stockholm.

The Instrument of Government (*Regeringsformen*), 1974:152.

Reports from Organizations

Ekonomistyrningsverket. (2013). Utfallet för statens budget – del av ESVs underlag för årsredovisning för staten 2012, ESV 2013:23, Stockholm.

OECD/International Transport Forum (ITF). (2008). *Transport Infrastructure Investment: Options for Efficiency.* Paris: OECD.

Trafikverket. (2012). Samhällsekonomiska principer och kalkylvärden för transportsektorn: ASEK 5.

B. Hasselgren, *Transport Infrastructure in Time, Scope and Scale*,
https://doi.org/10.1007/978-3-319-79054-1

Articles and Reports etc. by the Author

Hasselgren, B. (2011a). En mer effektiv transportinfrastruktur. *Ekonomisk Debatt, 39*(6), 20–34. Stockholm.

Hasselgren, B. (2011b). *The Reluctant Infrastructure Manager: Nationalization of Rail and Road Infrastructure in Sweden, 1930 to 1940*. Presented at Transportation Research Board's Annual Meeting 2012, USA.

Hasselgren, B. (2012a). *Effektivare transportinfrastruktur – med ny organization och finansiering*. Rapport för Stockholms Handelskammare 2012:1, Stockholm.

Hasselgren, B. (2013a). The Swedish Government as Owner of Transport Infrastructure. Policy Formation from the 1930s to the 2010s. *Scandinavian Journal of Public Administration, 16*(4), 49–71.

Hasselgren, B. (2013b). *The Reluctant Infrastructure Manager, 70 Years of Government Ownership of Transport Infrastructure in Sweden*. KTH Royal Institute of Technology, Research Paper, Stockholm.

Hasselgren, B. (2013c). *Näringslivets transporter, Hur kan transportinfrastrukturen bli mer effektiv?* Research Report for the Transport Group (*TransportGruppen*), ISSN 1653-6126, Stockholm.

Hasselgren, B. (2013d). *Transportinfrastrukturen i förändring, Organisering och finansiering*. ESO-rapport, juni 2013, Finansdepartementet, Stockholm.

Hasselgren, B. (2013e). Pricing Principles, Efficiency Concepts and Incentive Models in Swedish Transport Infrastructure Policy, Reprinted from VTI rapport 787, pp. 22–35, Swedish National Road and Transport Research Institute (VTI), Linköping.

Hasselgren, B. (2013f). Marginal Cost Controversies in Swedish Transport Infrastructure Policy, Aalborg University, Denmark.

Other Literature

Alexandersson, G. (2010). *The Accidental Deregulation: Essays on Reforms in the Swedish Bus and Railway Industries 1979–2009* (Doctoral Dissertation, Stockholm School of Economics).

Altschuler, A., & Luberoff, D. (2003). *Mega Projects—The Changing Politics of Urban Public Investments*. Washington, DC: The Brookings Institution.

Alvfors, K.-G. (1977). *Järnvägsförstatligandet - svensk järnvägspolitik under 1930-talet*. Svenska järnvägsklubbens skriftserie nr 21.

Andersson-Skog, L. (1993). *Såsom allmänna inrättningar till gagnet, men affärsföretag till namnet. SJ, järnvägspolitiken och den ekonomiska omvandlingen efter 1920*, Aa Umeå.

Andersson-Skog, L. (1996). From State Railway Housekeeping to Railway Economics, Swedish Railway Policy and Economic Transformation After 1920 in an Institutional Perspective. *Scandinavian Economic History Review, 44*(1), 23–42.

Anell L., Hedborg A., Lönnroth M., & Ingelstam L. (1971). *Ska vi asfaltera Sverige?* Pan/ Norstedts.

Banister, D. (2002). *Transport Planning*. London, UK: Routledge.

Banister, D., & Hickman, R. (2012). Transport Futures: Thinking the Unthinkable. *Transport Policy*. https://doi.org/10.1016/j.tranpol.2012.07.005.

Bas, D. S. (2011). Hayek's Critique of the General Theory: A New View of the Debate Between Hayek and Keynes. *The Quarterly Journal of Austrian Economics, 14*(3), 288–310.

Bergh van den, J., & Stagl, S. (2003). Coevolution of Economic Behavior and Institutions: Towards a Theory of Institutional Change. *Journal of Evolutionary Economics, 13*(3), 289–317.

Blankart, C. B., & Fasten, E. R. (2011). Knut Wicksell's Principle of Just Taxation Revisited. In V. Caspari (Ed.), *The Evolution of Economic Theory Essays in Honour of Bertram Schefold* (pp. 132–141). London: Routledge.

Blaug, M. (2007). The Fundamental Theories of Modern Welfare Economics, Historically Contemplated. *History of Political Economy, 39*(2), 185–207.

Blomkvist, P. (2001). *Den goda vägens vänner – Väg- och billobbyn och framväxten av det svenska bilsamhället 1914–1959*. Stockholm/Stehag: Brutus Östlings Bokförlag Symposion.

Bogart, D. (2009). Nationalizations and the Development of Transport Systems: Cross-Country Evidence from Railroad Networks, 1860–1912. *The Journal of Economic History, 69*(1), 202–237.

Bohm, P. (1973). Ansvarigt och oansvarigt om bilismens kostnader. *Ekonomisk Debatt, 1*(5), 326–330.

Bohm, P., Bruzelius, N., Hesselborn, P.-O., Johannesson, M., Ruud, T., & Thedéen, T. (1974). *Transportpolitiken och samhällsekonomin*. Stockholm: LiberFörlag.

Bruzelius, N., Flyvbjerg, B., & Rothengatter, W. (2002). Big Decisions, Big Risks. Improving Accountability in Mega Projects. *Transport Policy, 9*(2), 143–154.

Buchanan, J. M. (1968/1999). *The Demand and Supply of Public Goods*. USA: Liberty Fund Inc.

Buchanan, J. M., & Tullock, G. (1962). *The Calculus of Consent: Logical Foundations of Constitutional Democracy* (Vol. 100). Ann Arbor: University of Michigan Press.

Bulletinen. (2012). Nr 2, 2012, Enskild väghållning i svensk historia 1200–2010, based on Blomkvist, P. (2010) Om förvaltning av gemensamma resurser: Enskild väghållning och allmänningens dilemma i svensk historia 1200–2010 (Managing Common Pool Resources: Road Keeping and the Dilemma of the Commons in Swedish History 1200–2010), Division of Industrial Dynamics, Royal Institute of Technology, Stockholm (Stockholm 2010), TRITA- IEO 2010:06.

Button, K. (2010). Transportation Economics: Some Developments Over the Past 30 Years. *Journal of the Transportation Research Forum, 45*(2), 7–30.

Button, K. J., & Hensher, D. A. (2005). *Handbook of Transport Strategy, Policy and Institutions*. Oxford: Elsevier.

Chandler, A. D. (1977). *The Visible Hand: The Managerial Revolution in American Business*. Cambridge, MA, USA: The Belknap Press of Harvard University Press.

Chandler, A. D. (1990). *Scale and Scope: The Dynamics of Industrial Capitalism*. Cambridge, MA, USA: The Belknap Press of Harvard University Press.

Chandler, A. D. (1992). Capabilities and the Economic History of Industrial Enterprise. *The Journal of Economic Perspectives, 6*(3), 79–100.

Chisholm, D. (1989). *Coordination Without Hierarchy, Informal Structures in Multiorganizational Systems*. Berkeley: University of California Press.

Clifton, J., Lanthier, P., & Schröter, H. (2011). Regulating and Deregulating the Public Utilities 1830–2010. *Business History, 53*(5), 659–672.

Coase, R. H. (1937). The Nature of the Firm. *Economica, New Series, 4*(16), 386–405.

Coase, R. H. (1946). The Marginal Cost Controversy. *Economica, New Series, 13*(51), 169–182.

Coase, R. H. (1947). The Marginal Cost Controversy: Some Further Comments. *Economica, New Series, 14*(54), 150–153.

Coase, R. H. (1960). The Problem of Social Cost. *Journal of Law and Economics, 3*, 1–44.

Coase, R. H. (1970). The Theory of Public Utility Pricing and Its Application. *The Bell Journal of Economics and Management Science, 1*(1), 113–128.

Flyvbjerg, B. (1998). *Rationality and Power: Democracy in Practice*. Chicago and London: University of Chicago Press.

Flyvbjerg, B. (2007a). Policy and Planning for Large-Infrastructure Projects: Problems, Causes, Cures. *Environment and Planning: B Planing and Design, 34*(4), 578 ff.

Flyvbjerg, B. (2007b). Truth and Lies About Megaprojects. Inaugural Speech, TU Delft.

Glaeser, E. (2011). *Triumph of the City—How Our Greatest Invention Make Us Richer, Smarter, Greener, Healthier and Happier*. New York: Penguin Group.

Gruber, J. (2011). *Public Finance and Public Policy*. New York: Worth Publishers.

Harvey, D. (1989). *The Urban Experience*. UK: The John Hopkins University Press.

Hasselgren, B. (2013). *Government's Role for Transport Infrastructure—Theoretical Approaches and Historical Development*. PhD Dissertation, KTH Royal Insititute of Technolgy, Stockholm.

Hayek, F. A. (1944). *The Road to Serfdom, Text and Documents* (B. Caldwell, Ed. (2007)). Chicago: University of Chicago Press.

Hayek, F. A. (1945). The Use of Knowledge in Society. *American Economic Review, 35*(4), 519–530.

Hayek, F. A. (1960). *The Constitution of Liberty—The Definitive Edition* (R. Hamowy, Ed.(2011)). Chicago: University of Chicago Press.

Hayek, F. A. (1984). *Der Strom der Güter und Leistungen* (Vol. 101). Tübingen, Germany: Mohr Siebeck.

Heckscher, E. F. (1907). *Till belysning af jernvägarnas betydelse för Sveriges ekonomiska utveckling*. Stockholm: Centraltryckeriet.

Hernes, T. (2008). *Understanding Organization as Process—Theory for a Tangled World*. Oxon, UK: Routledge.

Hotelling, H. (1938). The General Welfare in Relation to Problems of Taxation and of Railway and Utility Rates. *Econometrica: Journal of the Econometric Society, 6*(3), 242–269.

Huerta de Soto, J. (2010). *The Austrian School*. Cheltenham, UK and Northampton, USA: Edward Elgar.

Hughes, T. P. (1987). Reverse Salients and Critical Problems: The Dynamics of Technological Change. In G. Dosi, R. Giannetti, & P. A. Toninelli (Eds.), *Technology and enterprise in a historical perspective*, 97–118. Oxford: Clarendon Press.

Hultén, J. (2012). *Nya vägar till järnvägar och vägar, Finansieringspragmatism och planeringsrationalism vid beslut om infrastrukturinvesteringar*, Political Studies 166. Lund.

Johnson, D., & Turner, C. (2007). *Strategy and Policy for Trans-European Networks*. Houndmills, Basingstoke, Hampshire: Palgrave Macmillan.

Kaijser, A. (1994). *I fädrens spår....* Stockholm: Carlssons Bokförlag.

Kaijser, A. (2004). The Dynamics of Infrasystems. Lessons from History. *Proceedings of the 6th International Summer Academy on Technology Studies—Urban Infrastructure in Transition.*

Klein, D. B. (2012). *Knowledge and Coordination—A Liberal Interpretation.* New York: Oxford University Press Inc.

Klein, P. G. (1998). New Institutional Economics. *Encyclopedia of Law and Economics, 1,* 456–489.

Kölbl, R., Niegl, M., & Knoflacher, H. (2008). A Strategic Planning Methodology. *Transport Policy, 15*(5), 273–282.

Laffont, J. J., & Tirole, J. (1993). *A Theory of Incentives in Procurement and Regulation.* Cambridge, USA: MIT Press.

Langlois, R. N. (1992). Transaction-Cost Economics in Real Time, *Industrial and Corporate Change, 1*(1), 99–127.

Langlois, R. N. (2003). *Chandler in a Larger Frame: Markets, Transaction Costs and Organizational Form in History* (Economics Working Paper No. 16). University of Connecticut.

Leflavie, X. (1996). Organization as Structures of Domination. *Organization Studies, 17*(1), 23–47.

Levinson, D. M. (2002). *Financing Transportation Networks.* Cheltenham: Edward Elgar.

Liljegren, E. (1999). *Den stora förvirringen. Partipolitik och bilintressen i riksdagsbehandlingen av bilskatternas utformning 1922–1939* (Working Papers in Transport and Communication History 1999:5). Sweden: Umeå University and Uppsala University.

Lindsey, R. (2006). Do Economists Reach A Conclusion on Road Pricing? The Intellectual History of an Idea. *Economic Journal Watch, 3*(2), 292–379.

March, J. G., & Simon, H. A. (1958). *Organizations.* New York: Wiley.

Matthiessen, C. W., Andersson, Å. E., & Andersson, D. E. (2013). *Öresundsregionen. Den dynamiska Metropolen.* Dialogos Förlag.

McCarthy, P. S. (2001). *Transportation Economics; Theory and Practice: A Case Study Approach.* Malden, MA: Blackwell.

McCloskey, N. D. (2010). *Bourgeois Dignity: Why Economics Can't Explain the Modern World.* Chicago, USA and London, UK: Chicago University Press.

McCraw, T. K. (2007). *Prophet of Innovation, Joseph Schumpeter and Creative Destruction.* Cambridge, MA and London, UK: Belknap Press of Harvard University Press.

Medema, S. G. (2009). *The Hesitant Hand, Taming Self-interest in the History of Economic Ideas.* Princeton, USA: Princeton University Press.

Merkert, R. (2009). *The Organization of European Railways: A Transaction Cost Perspective*. The University of Leeds Institute for Transport Studies.

Milgrom, P. R., & Roberts, J. (1992). *Economics, Organization and Management*. Englewood Cliffs, NJ: Prentice-Hall.

Millward, R. (2005). *Private and Public Enterprise in Europe*. UK: Cambridge University Press.

Millward, R. (2011). Public Enterprise in the Modern Western World: An Historical Analysis. *Annals of Public and Cooperative Economics, 82*(4), 378–398.

Mokyr, J. (1990). *The Lever of Riches: Technological Creativity and Economic Progress*. Oxford, UK: Oxford University Press.

Mosca, M. (2008). On the Origins of the Concept of Natural Monopoly: Economies of Scale and Competition. *The European Journal of the History of Economic Thought, 15*(2), 317–353.

Nelson, R., & Winter, S. (1982). *An Evolutionary Theory of Economic Change*. Cambridge, MA and London, UK: Belknap Press of Harvard University Press.

Newbery, D. M. (1990). Pricing and Congestion: Economic Principles Relevant to Pricing Roads. *Oxford Review of Economic Policy, 5*(2), 22–38.

North, D. C. (1990). *Institutions, Institutional Change and Economic Performance*. Cambridge, UK: Cambridge University Press.

Oates, W. E. (2005). Toward a Second-Generation Theory of Fiscal Federalism. *International Tax and Public Finance, 12*(4), 349–373.

Osborne, S. (Ed.). (2009). *The New Public Governance?: Emerging Perspectives on the Theory and Practice of Public Governance*. London and New York: Routledge.

Ostrom, E. (2005). *Understanding Institutional Diversity*. Princeton, NJ: Princeton University Press.

Ottosson, J. (1997). Path Dependence and Institutional Evolution: The Case of the Nationalisation of Private Railroads in Interwar Sweden. In L. Magnusson & J. Ottosson (Eds.), *Evolutionary Economics and Path Dependence* (pp. 186–196). Cheltenham: Edward Elgar.

Ottosson, J., & Andersson-Skog, L. (2013). *Stat, marknad och reglering i historiskt perspektiv*. Uppdragsforskningsrapport 2013:3. Swedish Competition Authority (*Konkurrensverket*), Stockholm.

Parry, I. W., & Bento, A. (2001). Revenue Recycling and the Welfare Effects of Road Pricing. *The Scandinavian Journal of Economics, 103*(4), 645–671.

Pennington, M. (2002). *Liberating the Land the Case for Private Land-Use Planning*. London: Institute for Economic Affairs.

Pennington, M. (2004). Citizen Participation, the 'Knowledge Problem' and Urban Land Use Planning: An Austrian Perspective. *The Review of Austrian Economics, 17*(2), 213–231.

Pennington, M. (2011). *Robust Political Economy, Classical Liberalism and the Future of Public Policy*. Cheltenham, UK: Edward Elgar

Peters, B. G., & Pierre, J. (2004). Multi-level Governance and Democracy: A Faustian Bargain? In I. Bache & M. Flinders (Eds.), *Multi-level Governance*. Oxford: Oxford University Press.

Pierson, P. (2000). Increasing Returns, Path Dependence and the Study of Politics. *The American Political Science Review, 94*(2), 251–267.

Raiffa, H., with Richardson, J., & Metcalfe, D. (2002). *Negotiation Analysis*. Cambridge, MA and London, UK: Harvard University Press.

Remmo, J. (2012). Utmaningar och hinder i gränsöverskridande transport-infrastrukturplanering: En studie av TEN-T med Nordiska triangeln som exempel (Master Thesis, KTH Royal Institute of Technology).

Rietveld, P. (2012). Barrier Effects of Borders: Implications for Borders; Implications for Border-Crossing Infrastructure. *European Journal for Transport Infrastructure and Research, 12*(2), 150–166.

Rietveld, P., & Stough, R. (2007). *Institutions and Sustainable Transport: Regulatory Reform in Advanced Economies*. Cheltenham, UK and Northhampton, USA: Edward Elgar.

Roth, G. (Ed.). (2006). *Street Smart, Competition, Entrepreneurship and the Future of Roads*. The Independent Institute, Transaction Publishers.

Ruggles, N. (1949). The Welfare Basis of the Marginal Cost Principle. *Review of Economic Studies, 17*(1), 29-46.

Ruiter, D. (2005). Is Transaction Cost Economics Applicable to Public Governance? *European Journal of Law and Economics, 20*(3), 287–303.

Sager, T. (2012). *Reviving Critical Planning Theory*. London: Routledge.

Samuelsson, P. A. (1954). The Pure Theory of Public Expenditure. *The Review of Economics and Statistics, 36*(4), 387–389.

Sannerstedt, A. (1979). *Fri konkurrens eller politisk styrning? 1963 års trafik-politiska beslut – debatten om innehåll, tillämpning och effekter*. Lund: Studentlitteratur.

Schön, D. A. (1971). *Beyond the Stable State: Public and Private Learning in a Changing Society*. London: Temple Smith.

Schumpeter, J. A. (1942/2008). *Capitalism, Socialism and Democracy*. New York: Harper Perennial Modern Thought.

Schumpeter, J. A. (1950) The March Into Socialism. *The American Economic Review, 40*(2), 446–456.

Short, J., & Kopp, A. (2005). Transport Infrastructure: Investment and Planning. Policy and Research Aspects. *Transport Policy, 12*(4), 360–367.

Thoresson, K. (2011). *Att beräkna det goda samhället: Samhällsekonomiska analyser och gränslandet expertis-politik inom transportområdet* (Doctoral Dissertation, Linköping).

Tiebout, C. (1956). A Pure Theory of Local Expenditures. *Journal of Political Economy, 64*(5), 416–424.

Tunzelmann von, N. (2003). Historical Co-evolution of Governance and Technology in the Industrial Revolutions. *Structural Change and Economic Dynamics, 14*(4), 365–384.

Van Wee, B. (2007). Large Infrastructure Projects: A Review of the Quality of Demand Forecasts and Cost Estimations. *Environment and Planning B: Planning and Design, 34*(4), 611–625.

Vickerman, R. (2007). *Recent Evolution of Research into the Wider Economic Benefits of Transport Infrastructure Investment* (OECD/ITF Joint Transport Research Centre Discussion Papers No. 2007/9). OECD Publishing.

Wagner, R. E. (Ed.). (1991/2011). *Charging for Government: User Charges and Earmarked Taxes in Principle and Practice*. New York, USA: Routledge Revivals.

Wagner, R. E. (2007). *Fiscal Sociology and the Theory of Public Finance—An Exploratory Essay*. Northampton: Edward Elgar.

Webster, C. (2002). Property Rights and the Public Realm: Gates, Green Belts and Gemeinschaft. *Environment and Planning B: Planning and Design, 29*(3), 312–397.

Williamson, O. E. (1981). The Economics of Organization: The Transaction Cost Approach. *The American Journal of Sociology, 87*(3), 548–577.

Williamson, O. E. (1999). Public and Private Bureaucracies: A Transaction Cost Economics Perspective. *The Journal of Law, Economics and Organization, 15*(1), 306–342.

Williamson, O. E. (2000). The New Institutional Economics: Taking Stock, Looking Ahead. *Journal of Economic Literature, 38*(3), 595–613.

Winston, C. (1991). Efficient Transportation Infrastructure Policy. *The Journal of Economic Perspectives, 5*(1), 113–127.

Winston, C. (2010). *Last Exit—Privatization and Deregulation of the U.S. Transportation System*. Washington, DC: Brookings Institution Press.

Zappia, C. (2001). Equilibrium and Disequilibrium Dynamics in the 1930s. *Journal of the History of Economic Thought, 23*(1), 55–75.

Index

A

Altschuler, A. 58
Andersson-Skog, L. 10, 11, 48, 83

B

Blaug, M. 33
Bogart, D. 4, 10, 48, 83
Bohm, P. 99

C

Chandler, A.D. 2, 10, 43, 47–49
Coase, R.H. 29, 38, 42, 65, 73, 75, 91–97, 101, 103
co-evolution xiii, 46, 79
co-evolutionary approach xiii–xv, 11, 14, 15, 25, 46, 47, 49, 50, 79, 80, 85, 90
concatenate coordination 61, 63
coordination xii, 3, 6, 11, 28, 49, 51, 57, 59–63, 67, 69–72, 74, 83, 84, 108
Core Network Corridors (CNSs) 3
cost responsibility principle 85, 97

D

deregulation xiv, 2, 11, 45, 48, 87, 88, 100

E

economics xiv, 3, 11, 12, 14, 18, 25, 26, 32, 34–36, 38, 40, 46, 50, 51, 58, 61, 65, 79, 80, 82, 87, 89, 92, 94, 96, 98–100

B. Hasselgren, *Transport Infrastructure in Time, Scope and Scale*,
https://doi.org/10.1007/978-3-319-79054-1

F
Flyvbjerg, B. 58
full cost coverage 50, 86, 90, 91, 93, 94, 96, 97, 99

G
government ownership xiii, xiv, 1–4, 79, 86, 88

H
Hayek, F.A. 28, 39, 40, 60, 65, 70, 73, 86, 93
Hotelling, H. 32, 33, 92, 94, 95

I
incentives 25, 41, 42, 47, 58, 92–94, 96, 101–103

K
Kaijser, A. 10, 47, 51
Klein, D.B. 5, 6, 29, 61–63, 73

L
Langlois, R.N. 43, 44, 46, 47, 60
liberalization 2, 11, 14, 88
Luberoff, D. 58, 72

M
marginal cost controversies 90, 92, 97, 102
Medema, S.G. 27, 29, 39
Millward, R. 2, 10, 12, 48, 49, 82, 83
Mokyr, J. 41
mutual coordination 61, 63

N
nationalization 2, 10, 13, 15, 26, 33, 39, 48, 65, 66, 79, 81–85, 88, 91, 92, 98
North, D.C. 40, 47, 66

O
Ottosson, J. 10, 11, 48, 51

P
Pigou 32, 33, 92, 95
planning xiv–xv, 3, 11–13, 16, 20, 21, 28, 29, 32, 51, 57–65, 67–74, 85, 87, 98–100, 107–108
politics and socio-culture 50, 84
Public Private Partnerships (PPP) 41, 45

R
regional growth 3, 4, 6
roads and railroads xii–xiv, 1, 10, 15–18, 26, 29, 33, 34, 46, 50, 59, 69, 82, 90, 91, 96, 100
Ruggles, N. 32, 36

S
Schumpeter, J.A. 28, 39, 40, 82, 86
social marginal cost 87, 91, 96–99, 101
spontaneous ordering 28, 63, 64, 66, 72–75

T

technology xii, 1, 3–6, 11, 17, 36, 39, 44, 46, 47, 49–51, 59, 69, 79, 80, 82, 84, 85, 89

TEN-T. *See* Trans-European Networks for Transport (TEN-T)

transaction cost xiv, 12, 27, 40–47, 49, 50, 66, 75

Trans-European Networks for Transport (TEN-T) 67, 69, 71, 89

transport infrastructure policy xi, xiv, 4, 6, 12, 13, 57, 58, 85, 86, 89, 91, 97, 98, 102

transport infrastructure systems 1, 3, 10–15, 17–19, 22, 32–34, 42, 43, 46, 48, 49, 57, 59, 64, 67, 68, 83, 84, 91, 101, 103, 108

W

Wagner, R.E. 26, 28, 31, 35, 38, 51, 103

Williamson, O.E. 25–26, 32, 41–43, 66

Winston, C. 37, 72, 74, 95, 96

CPSIA information can be obtained
at www.ICGtesting.com
Printed in the USA
LVOW13*1352220718
584566LV00007B/282/P

9 783319 790534